Patchwork Picnic

Simple-to-Piece Blocks That Celebrate the Outdoors

GRACEY LARSON

Martingale®
Create with Confidence

Patchwork Picnic:
Simple-to-Piece Blocks That Celebrate the Outdoors
© 2019 by Gracey Larson

Martingale®
19021 120th Ave. NE, Ste. 102
Bothell, WA 98011-9511 USA
ShopMartingale.com

Printed in China
24 23 22 21 20 19   8 7 6 5 4 3 2 1

Library of Congress Cataloging-in-Publication Data
is available upon request.

ISBN: 978-1-68356-010-4

MISSION STATEMENT

We empower makers who use fabric and yarn
to make life more enjoyable.

CREDITS

**PUBLISHER AND
CHIEF VISIONARY OFFICER**
Jennifer Erbe Keltner

CONTENT DIRECTOR
Karen Costello Soltys

DESIGN MANAGER
Adrienne Smitke

MANAGING EDITOR
Tina Cook

PRODUCTION MANAGER
Regina Girard

ACQUISITIONS EDITOR
Amelia Johanson

PHOTOGRAPHER
Brent Kane

TECHNICAL EDITOR
Nancy Mahoney

ILLUSTRATOR
Sandy Loi

COPY EDITOR
Durby Peterson

DEDICATION

*Dedicated to Jesus. Also dedicated to my dad and mom,
Don and Shelly; my sisters, Amy and Emily;
my brother, Zach; and my grandma, Rita Pickering.*

Contents

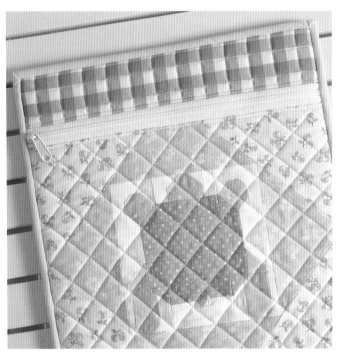

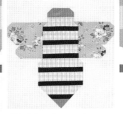

Introduction

I want to tell my story through the quilts that I make. My grandma, Rita Pickering, taught me how to quilt in 2009 with a basic sampler quilt, and I absolutely loved how each block had a different name and contained its own symbolism. Since that first quilt I have been drawn to sampler quilts because they give a unique opportunity to carry a message—to tell a story and share our adventures! As I have continued on my quilting journey, the desire to share events, memories, and symbols in my quilts has only grown, inspiring the patterns in this book. My hope is that these blocks help you tell your own story. The shapes and pictures contain images that we see all around us—things that often go unnoticed unless we take time to slow down and see the extraordinary beauty in the ordinary, such as a butterfly expanding its colorful wings or a quiet summer campfire.

Like many quilters, I wasn't always able to obtain fabric in large quantities, let alone stick to specific fabric collections, even though I loved and adored them. As they say, necessity is the mother of invention, and necessity led me on a scrap-happy adventure! Using fabrics from your own personal fabric stash, even bits and pieces, can lead to some of the most beautiful and unique masterpieces and really bring out a whole new level of creativity. These patterns will encourage you to use those beloved pieces that you've been hanging on to or to branch out and find new fabrics to try. No matter what fabrics you use, you'll finish a quilt that is completely unique.

And so, without further ado, let's go outside! Let's go spy on some beautiful bugs or go for a walk along the creek or in the garden—let's go on this quilting adventure together!

~ Gracey

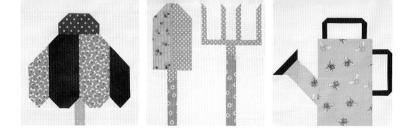

Tips, Tools, and Techniques

 One of the most exciting parts about the piecing method in this book is that you won't cut any triangles! You'll cut rectangles and squares, mark some pieces as directed, and stitch. This method is sometimes called the Stitch-and-Flip or Folded-Corner technique. It's so simple and it creates such fun and detailed designs. The method calls for using a ruler and pencil to mark the fabric pieces on the wrong side, drawing a diagonal line from corner to corner. You then place two pieces of fabric right sides together and sew along the marked line. See "Folded Corners" on page 7.

Several blocks in this book require small pieces. Working with small pieces is so much fun! Why? Because you can create shapes and designs you never thought you could create in a traditionally pieced block. Marking the pieces as instructed eliminates all the guesswork and makes it easy. The smaller pieces allow what would normally be blunt, pointed edges to become magically rounded (the eye in the Frog block, for example). You'll be so excited to see your blocks come together with this rounded-edge illusion that you just may end up binge sewing and ordering pizza for the family this week! Below are some tips that will make working with smaller pieces even easier.

TIPS FOR SEWING SMALL PIECES

◆ Take your time. It's OK to slow down and enjoy the process. Slowing down a bit will let you watch where the sewing-machine needle comes down, so you can make sure you're sewing on the marked line.

◆ Be very accurate when cutting and marking. As quilters we know this goes without saying, but accuracy becomes even more important when working with small pieces. Use a nonslip ruler and line it up exactly, using a rotary cutter to make a cutting a breeze.

◆ Keep your threads under control. When you're assembling multiple pieces it's amazing how many threads can stick out all over the place! Don't trim your threads too short, but as you sew, clip the threads that can get in the way or catch on your presser foot.

◆ Use a ¼" presser foot. This little tool has been a lifesaver for me. A ¼" foot is not necessary to make the blocks, as long as you can sew an accurate ¼" seam, but I've found it really helps me to sew accurately.

◆ Press the seam allowances open. While this is optional, pressing them open when working with many small pieces can help the block lie nice and flat. Stitch blocks together with the piece that has the most seams facing up. This way, you can make sure the seam allowances stay pressed open as you sew. They'll be easier to see, which makes sewing smoother.

◆ Use a mild quilting starch (I prefer Mary Ellen's Best Press) to help maintain accurate pressing and shape. Lightly starch the fabric before cutting, and then give seam allowances a light spritz as you go. This helps them stay pressed open and flat.

SUPPLIES AND TOOLS

All of the blocks in this book use traditional piecing methods—no paper foundation piecing or templates. (Yay!) While I appreciate paper piecing, it's just not my cup of tea. One thing I've always admired about paper piecing, however, is that it lets quilters create amazing pictures that normally couldn't be achieved otherwise. That is part of what led me on my journey of pattern design—creating pictures in quilt blocks using traditional methods that anyone can do. I love keeping things simple! All you'll need for this quilting adventure is the following: a sewing machine, fabric stash, rotary cutter, quilting rulers, a pencil (one for marking light fabric and one for marking dark), thread, and a way to label your pieces.

Each block contains multiple pieces, so organization is important. Every piece in each block is assigned a letter to help you keep track of which piece to use at any given time. Some great tools that I use to mark my fabric pieces are "Alphabitties" by It's Sew Emma, mini clothespins by Moda, or pieces of paper that I mark myself (although I prefer the first two options to save time).

FABRIC CHOICE

I love to think of fabric the way an artist looks at a paint palette. Something lovely happens when you start mixing colors and patterns in a way that's new and unique. The patterns in this book will encourage you to search through your own stash (and maybe shop for some new pieces—I mean, we'll never turn down the opportunity for more fabric, right?). Every block pattern has suggestions for colors to use, but I encourage you to explore your inner artist and mix some of your own "paint" (aka fabric choices).

With the exception of some of the patterns that are set at nighttime, for the majority of my blocks I use a traditional white background so the other colors pop. My personal favorite white fabric right now is Bella Solids White Bleached #9900-98 by Moda. When choosing my fabrics I like to keep it, as I call it, "controlled scrappy." I have so much fun mixing and matching fabrics but I prefer to keep like colors similar, if not the same. For example, once I decide on a specific shade of green, I use that same green in lots of different fabric pieces. I do the same with all the other colors. This controlled-scrappy method gives the projects a clean, cohesive look while still letting me be scrap-happy. In all of the projects, I have accounted for slightly more yardage than you'll actually need, so you'll have extra just in case. Let's get sewing!

FOLDED CORNERS

Mark, sew, trim, and press. That's all there is to turning squares and rectangles into units with diagonal seams!

1. Use an acrylic ruler and a fabric-marking pen or pencil to mark a diagonal line from corner to corner on the wrong side of the fabric. Make sure to mark *exactly* from the corner. You may need to scoot the ruler over a bit to allow for the width of your marking implement.

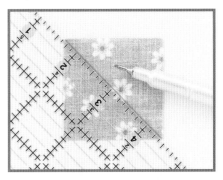

2. Place two fabrics right sides together as directed in the project and sew *exactly* on the marked line.

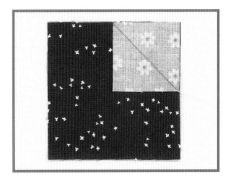

3. Fold open the top piece to make sure it's sewn accurately. If you're happy with the result, trim away the excess corner fabric leaving a ¼" seam allowance. Then press the top fabric open.

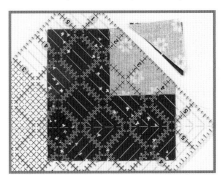

Sampler Quilt

DESIGNED AND MADE BY GRACEY LARSON; QUILTED BY ANNIE SEABOCH

Stitch all of your adventures together in one quilt and celebrate the simple pleasures and beauty of nature—in patchwork!

FINISHED SIZE: 69½" × 83" | BLOCK SIZE: 12" × 12"

MATERIALS

You'll need 30 blocks, 12" square. The quilt shown uses one of each of the block designs on pages 24–79. Yardage is based on 42"-wide fabric.

2½ yards of aqua solid for sashing and border
⅝ yard of brown print for binding
5⅛ yards of fabric for backing
78" × 91" piece of batting

CUTTING

All measurements include ¼"-wide seam allowances.

From the aqua solid, cut on the *lengthwise* grain:
2 strips, 2" × 80"
2 strips, 2" × 69½"
5 strips, 2" × 66½"
24 strips, 2" × 12½"

From the brown print, cut:
8 strips, 2¼" × 42"

ASSEMBLING THE QUILT TOP

Press the seam allowances in the directions indicated by the arrows. If you want to match the sampler quilt, see the quilt assembly diagram for the page numbers of the blocks.

1. Join five blocks and four aqua 2" × 12½" strips to make a block row that measures 12½" × 66½", including seam allowances. Make six rows.

2. Sew an aqua 2" × 66½" strip between each row to make the quilt-top center, which should measure 66½" × 80", including seam allowances.

3. Sew aqua 80"-long strips to the sides of the quilt top. Sew aqua 69½"-long strips to the top and bottom. The finished quilt top should measure 69½" × 83".

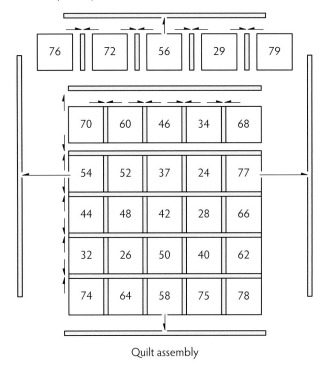

Quilt assembly

FINISHING THE QUILT

For more details on any of the finishing steps, visit ShopMartingale.com/HowtoQuilt to download free illustrated information.

1. Layer the backing, batting, and quilt top; baste.

2. Hand or machine quilt. The quilt shown is machine quilted with an allover design of swirls and loops.

3. Use the brown 2¼"-wide strips to make the binding; attach the binding to the quilt.

Matching Made Easy

To make sure all the blocks align in the finished quilt, measure and mark the long horizontal sashing strips. After allowing for the beginning ¼" seam allowance, mark off increments of 12", 1½", 12", 1½", and so on, along both long edges of the sashing. That way, you'll know exactly where to match the long sashing with the seam intersections of the block rows.

Picture Pot Holder

DESIGNED AND MADE BY GRACEY LARSON

Make cooking and baking more fun with custom pot holders. Pick a block, border, backing, and binding that coordinate with your kitchen, and even if your favorite meal is takeout, your kitchen will be pretty!

FINISHED SIZE: 7¼" × 8¼" | **BLOCK SIZE: 6" × 6"**

MATERIALS

You'll need 1 block, 6" square. (The Acorns block is on page 28, and the Coneflower block is on page 50.) Yardage is based on 42"-wide fabric. Fat quarters measure 18" × 21". Materials are for 1 Acorns pot holder.

⅓ yard of navy check for border, backing, and pocket lining
1 fat quarter of yellow print for pocket and hanging loop
¼ yard of navy solid for binding
20" × 20" square of Insul-Brite

CUTTING

All measurements include ¼"-wide seam allowances.

From the navy check, cut:
1 square, 9½" × 9½"
1 rectangle, 8½" × 9½"
2 strips, 1½" × 7½"
2 strips, 1" × 6½"

From the yellow print, cut:
1 square, 9½" × 9½"
1 rectangle, 2¼" × 4¼"

From the navy solid, cut:
1 strip, 2¼" × 42"
1 strip, 2¼" × 7¼"

From the Insul-Bright, cut:
2 squares, 9½" × 9½"
2 rectangles, 8½" × 9½"

MAKING THE POT HOLDER

For more detailed information on quilting and binding, visit ShopMartingale.com/HowtoQuilt. Seam allowances are ¼" except where otherwise indicated. Press the seam allowances open to reduce bulk.

1. Sew navy check 1" × 6½" strips to the sides of the block. Sew navy check 1½" × 7½" strips to the top and bottom to make the pot-holder front, which should measure 7½" × 8½".

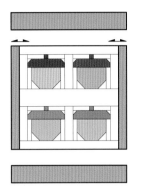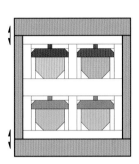

Make 1 unit, 7½" × 8½".

2. Place the navy check rectangle wrong side up on a flat surface. Layer two Insul-Brite rectangles (shiny side up) and the pot-holder front right side up; baste the layers together. Machine quilt straight lines to make a diagonal grid. Trim the quilted pot-holder front to measure 7¼" × 8¼", including seam allowances.

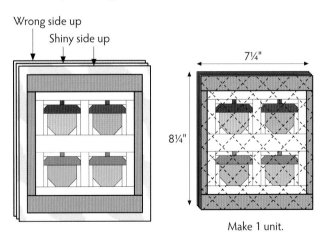

Make 1 unit.

3. Place the navy check square wrong side up on a flat surface. Layer two Insul-Brite squares (shiny side up) and the yellow square right side up on top of the navy check square; baste. Machine quilt straight lines to make a diagonal grid.

5. Position the pot-holder pocket, lining side down, on the back of the pot-holder front. Stitch the pocket to the pot holder along the side and bottom edges.

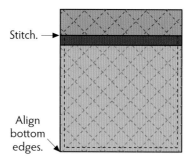

Stitch. →

Align bottom edges.

6. Fold the yellow rectangle in half lengthwise, wrong sides together, and press. Unfold, align the long raw edges with the center fold, and press. Refold on the center crease and topstitch to make the hanging loop.

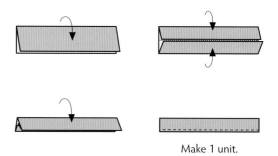

Make 1 unit.

7. Curve the loop piece into a U shape and center it on the back of the pot-holder front, aligning the raw edges with the top of the pot holder. Stitch the loop in place using a ⅛" seam allowance.

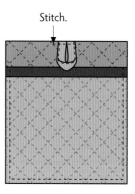

Stitch.

Add a Dash of Fun!

Choose colors to add flair and fun to your kitchen. If the navy color scheme used on the acorn pot holder isn't your jam, switch things up like I did for the Coneflower version above. You can even make a whole set of mix-and-match pot holders using the same color border fabric for all.

4. Trim the quilted square to measure 7" × 7¼", making sure the width of the quilted square matches the width of the quilted pot-holder front. Use the navy solid 2¼" × 7¼" strip to bind the top of the quilted square to make the pot-holder pocket.

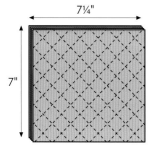

7¼"

7"

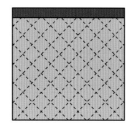

Make 1 unit.

8. Use the navy solid 2¼" × 42" strip to make the binding; attach the binding to the pot holder. Fold the hanging loop over the top edge of the pot holder and topstitch around the perimeter along the edge of the binding.

Songbird Table Runner

DESIGNED AND PIECED BY GRACEY LARSON; QUILTED BY ANNIE SEABOCH

Make your table setting sing with this colorful songbird table runner! You can keep the same bluebird color scheme as in the block pattern (page 24) or "branch" out and stitch a flock of beautiful, unique birds of all different colors. Be creative! This is a super easy project that you can make completely your own. If you're partial to a different quilt block entirely, replace the birds with the 6" block of your choice.

MATERIALS

You'll need 6 Bluebird blocks, 6" square, and 6 Four Patch blocks, which are made in the following project instructions. (The Bluebird block is on page 24.) Yardage is based on 42"-wide fabric.

½ yard of white solid for Four Patch blocks and border
¼ yard of aqua print for Four Patch blocks
¼ yard of pink diagonal stripe for binding
1⅓ yards of fabric for backing
22" × 46" piece of batting

CUTTING

All measurements include ¼"-wide seam allowances.

From the white solid, cut:
2 strips, 2" × 36½"
2 strips, 2" × 15½"
12 squares, 3½" × 3½"

From the aqua print, cut:
12 squares, 3½" × 3½"

From the pink diagonal stripe, cut:
3 strips, 2¼" × 42"

MAKING THE TABLE RUNNER

Press the seam allowances open to reduce bulk.

1. Join two white and two aqua squares to make a Four Patch block that measures 6½" square, including seam allowances. Make six blocks.

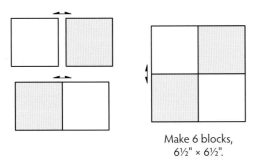

Make 6 blocks,
6½" × 6½".

2. Lay out the Bluebird and Four Patch blocks in two rows of six blocks each. Sew the blocks into rows. Join the rows to make the table-runner center, which should measure 12½" × 36½", including seam allowances.

3. Sew the white 36½" strips to the top and bottom of the table-runner center. Sew the white 15½" strips to the ends. The table runner should measure 15½" × 39½".

FINISHING THE TABLE RUNNER

For more details on any of the finishing steps, go to ShopMartingale.com/HowtoQuilt to download free illustrated information.

1. Layer the backing, batting, and table-runner top; baste.

2. Hand or machine quilt. The table runner shown is machine quilted with an allover design of four-leaf clovers.

3. Use the pink striped 2¼"-wide strips to make the binding; attach the binding to the table runner.

How Big Is Your Flock?

The table runner shown is just under 40" long. If you want a longer one, add more Four Patch blocks and birds. Why not make one bird for each person in your family? If you do extend the length, remember the you'll need more white solid and a bit bigger batting and backing.

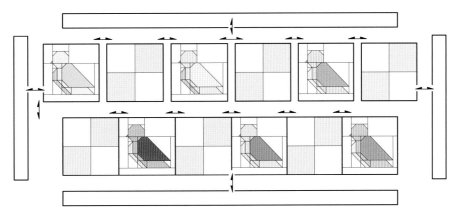

Table-runner assembly

Poppies Tote

DESIGNED AND MADE BY GRACEY LARSON

Display your favorite 6" block on this simple and quick sewing project. Use it on your day off to carry your journal, sketchbook, and a thermos of tea or coffee when you head out for a nature walk. It's perfect for workdays too. Stow your tablet, laptop, and everyday essentials for easy transport.

FINISHED SIZE: 13" × 15½"

MATERIALS

You'll need 1 block, 6" square. (The Poppies block is on page 60.) Yardage is based on 42"-wide fabric. Fat quarters measure 18" × 21".

⅛ yard of red dot for block border
½ yard of green gingham for tote body*
1 fat quarter of natural linen for tote base
½ yard of coordinating print for lining
¼ yard of black print for straps and button loop
22" × 42" piece of Soft and Stable**
1 wood button, 1½" diameter

If you want to match the checks along the seams of the tote, 1 yard of fabric is recommended.

** See "Soft and Stable" on page 21 to learn more about this product.*

CUTTING

All measurements include ¼"-wide seam allowances.

From the red dot, cut:
2 rectangles, 1½" × 8½"
2 rectangles, 1½" × 6½"

From the green gingham, cut:
2 rectangles, 4¾" × 8½"
1 rectangle, 2½" × 17"
1 rectangle, 2¾" × 17"
1 rectangle, 12¾" × 17"

From the natural linen, cut:
1 rectangle, 9½" × 17"

From the lining print, cut:
2 rectangles, 16" × 17¼"

From the black print, cut:
2 strips, 4" × 27"
1 rectangle, 1" × 7"

From the Soft and Stable, cut:
1 rectangle, 18" × 40"
2 strips, 1" × 27"

MAKING THE TOTE

For more detailed information on quilting and binding, visit ShopMartingale.com/HowtoQuilt. Seam allowances are ¼" except where otherwise indicated. Press the seam allowances in the directions indicated by the arrows.

1. Sew red 1½" × 6½" rectangles to the sides of the block. Sew red 1½" × 8½" rectangles to the top and bottom to make the block unit, which should measure 8½" square, including seam allowances.

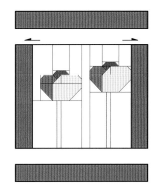
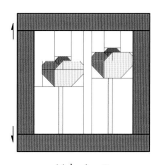

Make 1 unit,
8½" × 8½".

2. Sew green 4¾" × 8½" rectangles to the sides of the block unit. Sew the green 2½" × 17" rectangle to the top and the green 2¾" × 17" rectangle to the bottom to make the bag front, which should measure 17" × 12¾", including seam allowances.

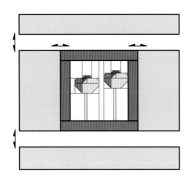

Make 1 unit,
17" × 12¾".

3. Join the bag front, linen rectangle, and green 12¾" × 17" rectangle to make the outer bag, which should measure 17" × 34", including seam allowances.

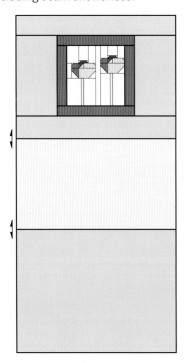

Make 1 unit,
17" × 34".

4. Layer the 18" × 40" rectangle of Soft and Stable on the wrong side of the outer bag; baste. Machine quilt with straight lines to form a diagonal grid. Trim the piece to measure 16½" × 34", including seam allowances.

5. Fold the quilted bag in half, right sides together, matching the side edges. Sew both side seams of the bag using a ½" seam allowance.

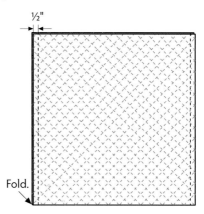

6. Place the lining rectangles right sides together. Sew the side and bottom edges, leaving a 4" gap at the bottom. Make sure to backstitch before and after the gap for extra strength. Do not sew along the top edge.

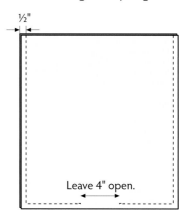

7. With wrong sides out, fold the bottom corners of the outer bag, aligning the side and bottom seams. On each corner, measure 1" from the point and draw a line perpendicular to the seam. Stitch on the marked line on both corners and trim ½" from the line to box the corners. Repeat on the corners of the lining.

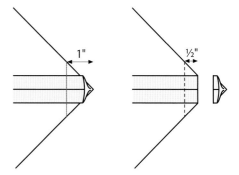

8. To make the straps, fold a black 4"-wide strip in half lengthwise, wrong sides together, and press. Unfold, turn the raw edges of the strip in to the center crease, and press the strip. On the wrong side, place a 1" × 27" strip of Soft and Stable on half of the strip. Fold the other half of the strip over to enclose the Soft and Stable. Topstitch along each long side of the strap, ⅛" from the edge. Repeat with the remaining black strip.

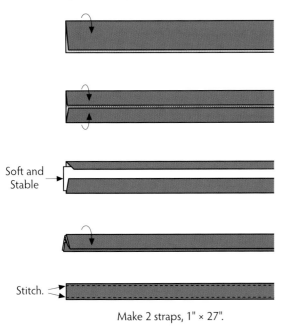

Soft and Stable

Stitch.

Make 2 straps, 1" × 27".

9. To make the button loop, fold the black 1" × 7" rectangle in half lengthwise, wrong sides together, and press. Unfold, turn the raw edges of the strip in to the center fold, refold on the center crease, and then press the strip. Topstitch along the folded edges.

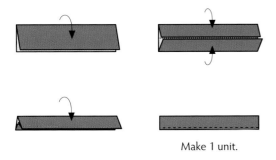

Make 1 unit.

10. Turn the bag right side out. Mark 2" in from each side seam along the top edge of the outer bag. With the raw edges matching, pin the ends of a strap to the bag, aligning the outer edges of the strap with the 2" marks. Repeat with the remaining strap on the other side of the bag. Sew the

button to the bag front, placing the top of the button ¾" from the top of the bag. Center and pin the button loop on the bag back, aligning the raw edges.

Center button placement

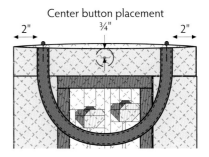

Center button loop.

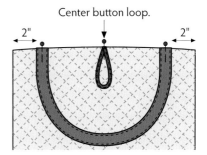

11. With right sides together, place the outer bag and straps inside the lining bag, sandwiching the straps between the layers. Align and pin the raw edges. Sew all the way around the top of the bag; backstitch at the start and end as well as over the straps for added durability.

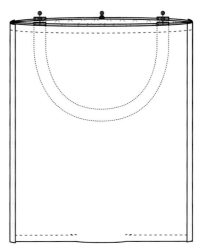

12. Pull the bag through the gap in the lining. Hand or machine stitch the gap closed. Push the lining down into the bag. Roll the top seam so about ¼" of lining shows on the outer bag; press. Topstitch around the top edge to finish the bag and keep the lining in place.

Packing Pouches

DESIGNED AND MADE BY GRACEY LARSON

Organize everything you need for your next trip with these packing pouches! The large one is roomy enough for a 15" laptop. The medium pouch holds chargers, cosmetics, and countless other items. The small pouch is perfect for jewelry, on-the-go sewing notions, or anything else that needs a home in your bag.

FINISHED SIZES: LARGE: 16½" × 13½"
MEDIUM: 12½" × 13½" | SMALL: 8½" × 9½"

MATERIALS

You'll need 2 blocks, 6" square, for the large pouch, and 1 block, 6" square, for each of the medium and small pouches. (The Tulip, Wildflower, Turtle, and Honeybee blocks are on pages 56, 76, 64, and 79, respectively.)

Large Pouch

8 squares, 2½" × 2½", of white solid for pouch front
8 squares, 2½" × 2½", of assorted prints for pouch front
1 rectangle, 2" × 6½", of white dot for pouch front
2 rectangles, 1¾" × 6½", of white dot for pouch front
1 rectangle, 4½" × 18", of fabric for lining (C)
1 rectangle, 4½" × 18", of white floral for pouch front (G)
1 rectangle, 12½" × 18", of fabric for lining (A)
1 rectangle, 15" × 18", of fabric for lining (B)
1 rectangle, 15" × 18", of coordinating fabric for
    pouch back (H)
2 strips, 2¼" × 42", of green dot for binding
1 rectangle, 4½" × 18", of Soft and Stable (F)
1 rectangle, 12½" × 18", of Soft and Stable (D)
1 rectangle, 15" × 18", of Soft and Stable (E)
1 nylon zipper, 20" long

Medium Pouch

2 rectangles, 3½" × 6½", of yellow print for pouch front
2 rectangles, 2½" × 12½", of yellow print for pouch front
4 squares, 5½" × 5½", of white floral for pouch front
1 rectangle, 4½" × 14", of fabric for lining (C)
1 rectangle, 4½" × 14", of green check for pouch front (G)
1 rectangle, 12½" × 14", of fabric for lining (A)
1 rectangle, 14" × 15", of fabric for lining (B)
1 rectangle, 14" × 15", of coordinating fabric for
    pouch back (H)
2 strips, 2¼" × 42", of yellow solid for binding
1 rectangle, 4½" × 14", of Soft and Stable (F)
1 rectangle, 12½" × 14", of Soft and Stable (D)
1 rectangle, 14" × 15", of Soft and Stable (E)
1 nylon zipper, 16" long

Small Pouch

2 rectangles, 1½" × 6½", of white solid for pouch front
1 rectangle, 4½" × 10", of fabric for lining (C)
1 rectangle, 4½" × 10", of yellow floral for pouch front (G)
1 rectangle, 8½" × 10", of fabric for lining (A)
1 rectangle, 10" × 11", of fabric for lining (B)
1 rectangle, 10" × 11", of coordinating fabric for
    pouch back (H)
2 strips, 2¼" × 42", of pink solid for binding
1 rectangle, 8½" × 10", of Soft and Stable (D)
1 rectangle, 10" × 11", of Soft and Stable (E)
1 rectangle, 4½" × 10", of Soft and Stable (F)
1 nylon zipper, 10" long

Soft and Stable

ByAnnie's Soft and Stable takes the place of batting or other stabilizers. Lightweight and easy to sew through, it provides lasting body and stability. Soft and Stable is available at many retail shops or online at byannie.com.

MAKING THE POUCH FRONT

After layering pieces marked with a diagonal line, stitch on the marked line. Seam allowances are ¼" except where otherwise indicated. Press the seam allowances in the directions indicated by the arrows.

Large Pouch

1. Join four white solid and four print 2½" squares to make a row that measures 2½" × 16½", including seam allowances. Make two rows.

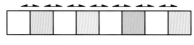

Make 2 units, 2½" × 16½".

2. Sew the white dot 2" × 6½" rectangle between the blocks. Sew white dot 1¾" × 6½" rectangles to the left and right sides of the blocks to make the middle row, which should measure 6½" × 16½", including seam allowances.

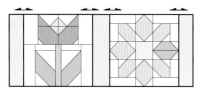

Make 1 unit, 6½" × 16½".

3. Join the rows from step 1 to the middle row to make the bottom section of the pouch front, which should measure 10½" × 16½", including seam allowances.

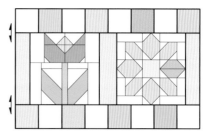

Make 1 unit, 10½" × 16½".

Medium Pouch

1. Sew yellow 3½" × 6½" rectangles to the sides of the block. Sew yellow 2½" × 12½" rectangles to the top and bottom to make a unit that measures 10½" × 12½", including seam allowances.

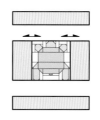

Make 1 unit,
10½" × 12½".

2. Draw a diagonal line on the wrong side of the white floral squares. Layer marked squares on opposite corners of the unit and stitch on the marked line. Trim the seam allowances to ¼" and press. Repeat to sew two squares on the remaining corners to make the bottom section of the pouch front, which should measure 10½" × 12½", including seam allowances.

 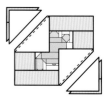

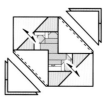

Make 1 unit,
10½" × 12½".

Small Pouch

Join white 1½" × 6½" rectangles to the sides of the block to make the bottom section of the pouch front, which should measure 6½" × 8½", including seam allowances.

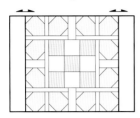

Make 1 unit,
6½" × 8½".

ASSEMBLING THE POUCH

For more detailed information on quilting and binding, visit ShopMartingale.com/HowtoQuilt.

1. Layer C, F, and G pieces, wrong sides together; baste. Machine quilt with straight lines to form a grid. Trim the quilted strip to measure 2½" × 16½" (large), 2½" × 12½" (medium), and 2½" × 8½" (small).

2. Layer A, D, and the bottom section of the pouch front, wrong sides together; baste. Machine quilt in a diagonal grid. Trim A and D even with the pouch front. The bottom section of the pouch front should measure 10½" × 16½" (large), 10½" × 12½" (medium), and 6½" × 8½" (small).

3. Place the zipper along the top edge of the bottom section of the pouch front, right sides together. Sew along the edge of the zipper, using a ¼" seam allowance. Press the seam allowances toward the pouch front. Topstitch along the edge of the seam so the zipper lies flat.

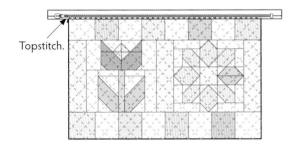

Topstitch.

4. Repeat step 3 with the quilted strip on the opposite side of the zipper, aligning the sides of the strip with the sides of the bottom section. Sew along the edge of the zipper.

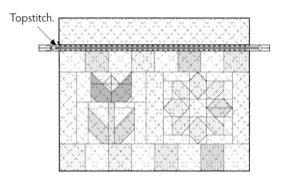

Topstitch.

5. Unzip the zipper so that the pull is in the middle of the pouch. Stitch across both ends of the zipper, ⅛" from the edge of the pouch. Trim the excess zipper.

Stitch.

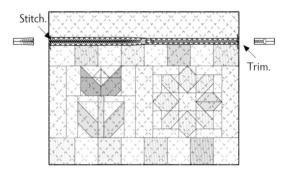

Trim.

6. Layer B, E, and H, wrong sides together. Machine quilt the pouch back in a grid. Using the pouch front as a guide, trim the pouch back to same size.

7. Pin the pouch front on top of the pouch back, wrong sides together. Stitch around the perimeter of the pouch. Use the 2¼"-wide strips to make the binding; attach the binding to the pouch.

Stitch.

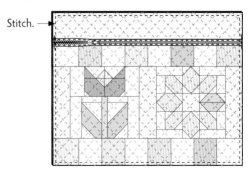

Bluebird

FABRIC	PIECE	6" BLOCK	12" BLOCK
Background (white)	A	1 rectangle, 1½" × 2½"	1 rectangle, 2½" × 4½"
	B	1 rectangle, 1¼" × 2¼"	1 rectangle, 2" × 4"
	C	5 squares, 1" × 1"	5 squares, 1½" × 1½"
	D	1 rectangle, 2½" × 3¾"	1 rectangle, 4½" × 7"
	E	1 square, 1¼" × 1¼"	1 square, 2" × 2"
	F	1 rectangle, 1½" × 3¾"	1 rectangle, 2½" × 7"
	G	1 square, 3" × 3"	1 square, 5½" × 5½"
	H	1 rectangle, 1" × 3¾"	1 rectangle, 1½" × 7"
	I	1 rectangle, 1¼" × 6½"	1 rectangle, 2" × 12½"
	J	1 rectangle, 1½" × 2"	1 rectangle, 2½" × 3½"
Bird body (light blue)	K	1 rectangle, 1" × 1½"	1 rectangle, 1½" × 2½"
	L	1 rectangle, 1" × 1¾"	1 rectangle, 1½" × 3"
	M	2 squares, 1" × 1"	2 squares, 1½" × 1½"
	N	2 squares, 1¼" × 1¼"	2 squares, 2" × 2"
	O	1 rectangle, 1¼" × 3"	1 rectangle, 2" × 5½"
	P	1 rectangle, 1¾" × 2¼"	1 rectangle, 3" × 4"
Bird belly (orange)	Q	1 rectangle, 1" × 1¾"	1 rectangle, 1½" × 3"
	R	1 square, 1½" × 1½"	1 square, 2½" × 2½"
	S	1 square, ¾" × ¾"	1 square, 1" × 1"
	T	1 rectangle, 1¼" × 1½"	1 rectangle, 2" × 2½"
Beak (orange solid)	U	1 square, ¾" × ¾"	1 square, 1" × 1"
Bird wing (medium blue)	V	1 rectangle, 3" × 4"	1 rectangle, 5½" × 7½"

MAKING THE BLOCK

Instructions are for both 6" and 12" blocks. Sew all pieces right sides together. When layering pieces marked with a diagonal line, stitch on the marked line. Trim the seam allowances to ¼". Press all seam allowances open to reduce bulk.

1. Draw a diagonal line on the wrong side of the C squares. Sew C to the top-left and top-right corners of P. Join B to P to make the head unit.

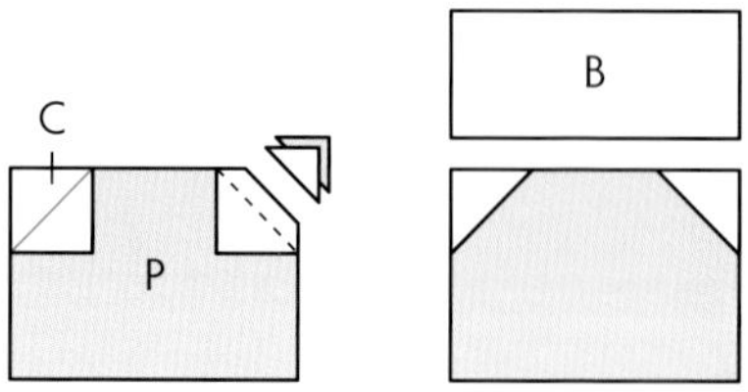

Make 1 unit.

2. Draw a diagonal line on the wrong side of U. Sew U to the bottom-right corner of A to make the A unit.

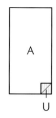
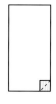
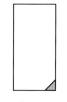

Make 1 unit.

3. Join the A unit, head unit, and D to make the top-bird unit.

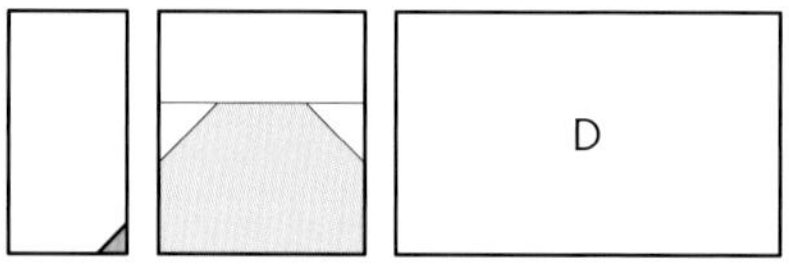

Make 1 unit.

4. Sew C to the left end of K to make the K unit.

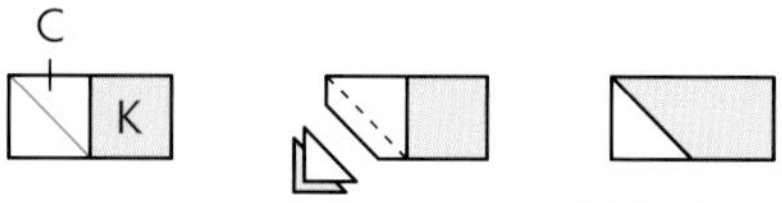

Make 1 unit.

5. Join Q to L to make the Q unit. Sew C to the top-left corner of the Q unit.

Make 1 unit.

6. Draw a diagonal line on the wrong side of the M and R squares. Sew R to the top-right corner of J. Sew M in the same manner to make the J unit.

Make 1 unit.

7. Join F and the K, Q, and J units to make the belly unit.

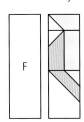 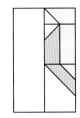

Make 1 unit.

8. Draw a diagonal line on the wrong side of the N squares. Sew N to the right end of T. Sew C to the bottom-left corner of T to make the T unit.

Make 1 unit.

9. Draw a diagonal line on the wrong side of E. Sew E to the right end of O to make the O unit.

Make 1 unit.

10. Join the T and O units to make the tail-feather unit.

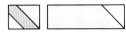

Make 1 unit.

11. Draw a diagonal line on the wrong side of the G and S squares. Sew G to the right end of V. Sew M to the top-left corner and N to the bottom-left corner of V. In the same

manner, sew S to the bottom-left corner of N to make the V unit.

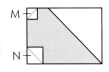

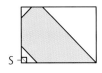

Make 1 unit.

12. Sew unit V to the tail-feather unit. Add H to make the wing unit. Join the belly and wing units to make the body unit.

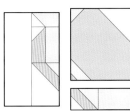

Make 1 unit.

13. Join the top-bird unit, body unit, and I to make the block.

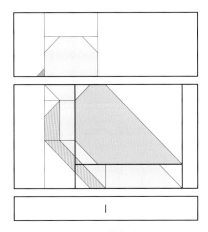

Bluebird block

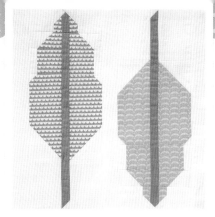

Feathers

FABRIC	PIECE	6" BLOCK	12" BLOCK
Background (white)	A	4 squares, 1¼" × 1¼"	4 squares, 2" × 2"
	B	3 rectangles, 1" × 6½"	3 rectangles, 1½" × 12½"
	C	8 squares, 1" × 1"	8 squares, 1½" × 1½"
	D	4 rectangles, ¾" × 1"	4 rectangles, 1" × 1½"
	E	4 rectangles, ¾" × 1¼"	4 rectangles, 1" × 2"
	F	6 squares, ¾" × ¾"	6 squares, 1" × 1"
	G	4 squares, 1½" × 1½"	4 squares, 2½" × 2½"
	H	4 rectangles, 1½" × 2"	4 rectangles, 2½" × 3½"
Feather centers (gray)	I	2 rectangles, ¾" × 1¼"	2 rectangles, 1" × 2"
	J	2 rectangles, ¾" × 5¾"	2 rectangles, 1" × 11"
Feathers (pink and blue)	K	4 rectangles, ¾" × 1¼" (2 pink, 2 blue)	4 rectangles, 1" × 2" (2 pink, 2 blue)
	L	4 rectangles, 1" × 1¼" (2 pink, 2 blue)	4 rectangles, 1½" × 2" (2 pink, 2 blue)
	M	4 squares, 1¼" × 1¼" (2 pink, 2 blue)	4 squares, 2" × 2" (2 pink, 2 blue)
	N	4 rectangles, 1½" × 3" (2 pink, 2 blue)	4 rectangles, 2½" × 5½" (2 pink, 2 blue)

MAKING THE BLOCK

Instructions are for both 6" and 12" blocks. Sew all pieces right sides together. When layering pieces marked with a diagonal line, stitch on the marked line. Trim the seam allowances to ¼". Press all seam allowances open to reduce bulk.

1. Sew I between two pink K rectangles to make an I unit. Repeat to make a blue I unit.

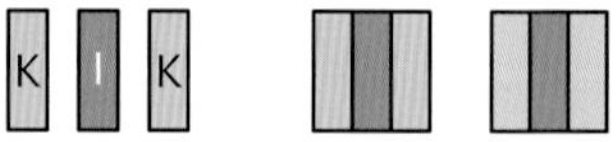

Make 1 of each unit.

2. Draw a diagonal line on the wrong side of the C squares. Sew C to the top-left and top-right corners of each I unit.

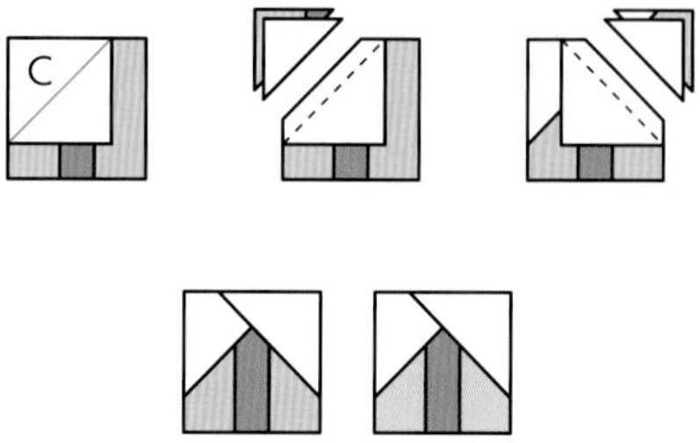

Make 1 of each unit.

3. Join two A squares to each I unit to make two feather-tip units.

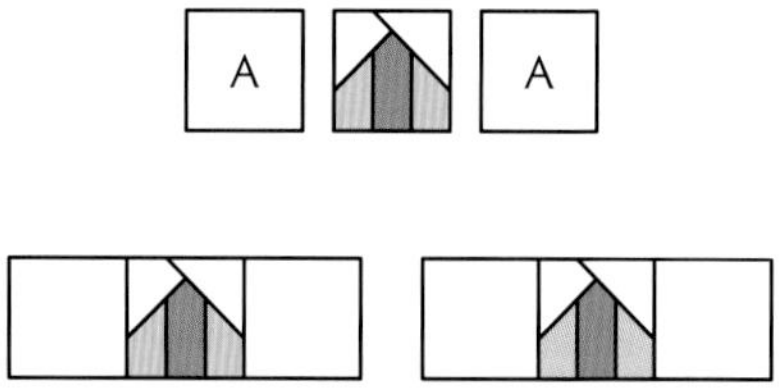

Make 1 of each unit.

4. Sew C to the left end of a pink L. Sew C to the right end of another pink L. Make one of each unit using the blue L rectangles.

Make 1 of each unit.

5. Join a D to each pink and blue L unit.

Make 1 of each unit.

Make 1 of each unit.

6. Join an E to each pink and blue M. Make two of each M unit.

Make 2 of each unit.

7. Draw a diagonal line on the wrong side of the F and G squares. Sew F to the top-left corner and G to the bottom-left corner of a pink N. Sew F to the top-right corner and G to the bottom-right corner of the other pink N. Sew F and G to the two blue N rectangles. Make one of each N unit.

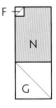 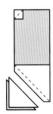

Make 1 of each unit.

8. Join the left pink L, M, and N units; add H to make the left pink-feather unit. Join the right pink L, M, and N units and H to make the right pink-feather unit. Repeat to make the left and right blue-feather units.

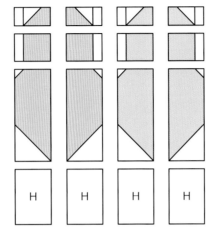

Make 1 of each unit.

9. Sew F to one end of J. Make two J units.

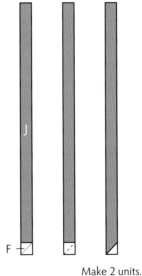

Make 2 units.

10. Sew a J unit between the pink units. Add the pink feather-tip unit to make the pink feather. In the same manner, join the blue units to a J unit; add the blue feather-tip unit to make the blue feather.

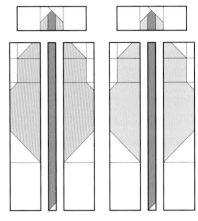

Make 1 of each unit.

11. Join three B rectangles and the pink and blue feathers to make the block. Note that the feathers point in opposite directions.

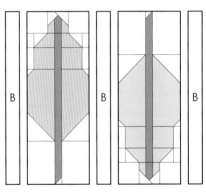

Feathers block

Acorns

FABRIC	PIECE	6" BLOCK	12" BLOCK
Background (white)	A	2 rectangles, 1" × 6½"	2 rectangles, 1½" × 12½"
	B	1 rectangle, 1½" × 6½"	1 rectangle, 2½" × 12½"
	C	6 rectangles, 1" × 2½"	6 rectangles, 1½" × 4½"
	D	8 rectangles, ¾" × 1½"	8 rectangles, 1" × 2½"
	E	8 squares, ¾" × ¾"	8 squares, 1" × 1"
	F	8 squares, 1" × 1"	8 squares, 1½" × 1½"
	G	8 rectangles, ¾" × 1¾"	8 rectangles, 1" × 3"
Acorns (2 browns, 1 orange, and 1 green)	H	4 rectangles, 1¾" × 2¼"	4 rectangles, 3" × 4"
Acorn tops (4 dark browns)	I	4 squares, ¾" × ¾"	4 squares, 1" × 1"
	J	4 rectangles, 1" × 2¾"	4 rectangles, 1½" × 5"

MAKING THE BLOCK

Instructions are for both 6" and 12" blocks. Sew all pieces right sides together. When layering pieces marked with a diagonal line, stitch on the marked line. Trim the seam allowances to ¼". Press all seam allowances open to reduce bulk.

1. Draw a diagonal line on the wrong side of the F squares. Sew F to the bottom-left and bottom-right corners of H. Make four units. Sew G

rectangles to each end of all units to make the acorn bottom.

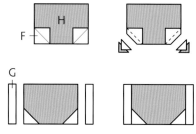

Make 4 units.

2. Draw a diagonal line on the wrong side of the E squares. Sew E to the

top-left and top-right corners of J to make four J units.

Make 4 units.

3. Sew I between two D rectangles. Make four acorn top units.

Make 4 units.

4. Join an acorn top, a J unit, and an acorn bottom to make the acorn unit. Make four units.

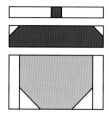

Make 4 units.

5. Join two acorn units and three C rectangles to make an acorn row. Make two rows.

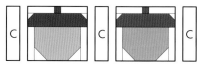

Make 2 rows.

6. Join two A, one B, and two acorn rows to make the block.

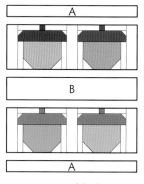

Acorns block

FABRIC	PIECE	6" BLOCK	12" BLOCK
Background (white)	A	1 rectangle, 1¾" × 6½"	1 rectangle, 3" × 12½"
	B	1 rectangle, 1" × 3½"	1 rectangle, 1½" × 6½"
	C	1 rectangle, 1¼" × 3½"	1 rectangle, 2" × 6½"
	D	1 rectangle, ¾" × 2½"	1 rectangle, 1" × 4½"
	E	11 squares, ¾" × ¾"	11 squares, 1" × 1"
	F	1 rectangle, ¾" × 2¼"	1 rectangle, 1" × 4"
	G	2 squares, 1" × 1"	2 squares, 1½" × 1½"
	H	1 rectangle, ¾" × 4½"	1 rectangle, 1" × 8½"
	I	1 rectangle, 1¼" × 2"	1 rectangle, 2" × 3½"
	J	1 rectangle, 1¼" × 2¼"	1 rectangle, 2" × 4"
	K	1 rectangle, 1¼" × 1½"	1 rectangle, 2" × 2½"
Grass (green)	L	1 rectangle, ¾" × 6½"	1 rectangle, 1" × 12½"
Bear body, nose, and ears (black)	M	4 squares, 1" × 1"	4 squares, 1½" × 1½"
	N	1 rectangle, 1" × 2"	1 rectangle, 1½" × 3½"
	O	1 rectangle, ¾" × 1½"	1 rectangle, 1" × 2½"
	P	1 rectangle, 2" × 2½"	1 rectangle, 3½" × 4½"
	Q	1 rectangle, 1½" × 3½"	1 rectangle, 2½" × 6½"
	R	1 square, ¾" × ¾"	1 square, 1" × 1"
	S	1 rectangle, ¾" × 1"	1 rectangle, 1" × 1½"
Bear legs and face (gray)	T	1 rectangle, ¾" × 2½"	1 rectangle, 1" × 4½"
	U	1 rectangle, 1¼" × 3"	1 rectangle, 2" × 5½"
	V	4 squares, ¾" × ¾"	4 squares, 1" × 1"
	W	2 rectangles, 1¼" × 1½"	2 rectangles, 2" × 2½"
	X	1 rectangle, 1½" × 1¾"	1 rectangle, 2½" × 3"
	Y	1 square, 2" × 2"	1 square, 3½" × 3½"
	Z	1 rectangle, 1¼" × 2¼"	1 rectangle, 2" × 4"
	AA	1 rectangle, 1¼" × 1¾"	1 rectangle, 2" × 3"
	BB	1 rectangle, 1" × 1½"	1 rectangle, 1½" × 2½"
Bear snout (brown)	CC	3 rectangles, ¾" × 1"	3 rectangles, 1" × 1½"
	DD	2 squares, ¾" × ¾"	2 squares, 1" × 1"

MAKING THE BLOCK

Instructions are for both 6" and 12" blocks. Sew all pieces right sides together. When layering pieces marked with a diagonal line, stitch on the marked line. Trim the seam allowances to ¼". Press all seam allowances open to reduce bulk.

1. Draw a diagonal line on the wrong side of the E and V squares. Sew E to the top-left corner of an M. Sew E to the top-right and bottom-left corners of M. Sew V to the bottom-right corner of M. Make two M units.

Make 2 units.

2. Join D and T to make the D unit.

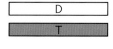

Make 1 unit.

3. Join the M units, D unit, and B to make the ear unit. Sew A to the unit to make the top-bear unit.

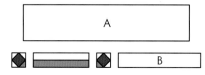

Make 1 unit.

4. Draw a diagonal line on the wrong side of the G squares. Sew G to the top-right corner of Q. Sew C to Q to make the bear-back unit.

Make 1 unit.

5. Draw a diagonal line on the wrong side of the DD squares. Sew DD to the left and right ends of S to make the S unit.

6. Join CC rectangles to the S unit. Sew BB to the S unit to make the nose unit.

Make 1 unit.

7. Sew V to the top-left and top-right corners of the nose unit.

Make 1 unit.

8. Sew W and U rectangles to the nose unit to make the face unit.

Make 1 unit.

9. Draw a diagonal line on the wrong side of the remaining M squares. Sew M to the bottom-right corner and a marked G to the bottom-left corner of the face unit.

 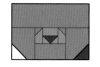

Make 1 unit.

10. Join F, the face unit, and the bear-back unit to make the body unit.

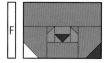 

Make 1 unit.

11. Sew E to the bottom-left corner of N to make the N unit.

Make 1 unit.

12. Draw a diagonal line on the wrong side of R. Sew R to the top-left corner of X. Sew O to X to make the X unit.

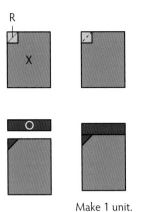

Make 1 unit.

13. Join I, unit N, and unit X to make the front-leg unit.

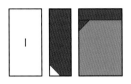

Make 1 unit.

14. Sew M to the top-left corner of Y. Join P to Y to make the back-leg unit.

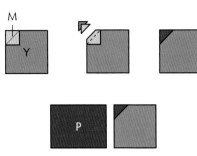

Make 1 unit.

15. Join the back-leg and front-leg units to complete the leg unit.

Make 1 unit.

16. Sew E to the top-left and bottom-right corners of AA. Sew E to Z. Make one of each unit.

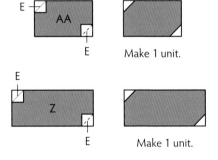

Make 1 unit.

Make 1 unit.

17. Join K, the AA unit, J, and the Z unit to make the feet unit.

Make 1 unit.

18. Join the body, leg, and feet units to make the bear body. Join H to the bear body. Join the top-bear unit, the bear body, and L to make the block.

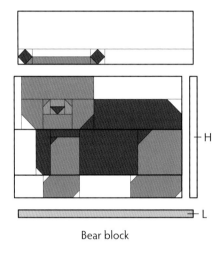

Bear block

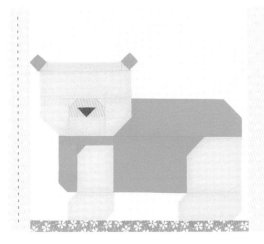

What Color Is Your Bear?

Not all bears are black! While you wouldn't want a grizzly bear to visit your picnic, you could use warm brown tones for your bear and call him Teddy. Or make him even more colorful, like a stuffed bear. Just make sure to have some value contrast between the body color and that used for the legs and head.

Good Night

FABRIC	PIECE	6" BLOCK	12" BLOCK
Background (black)	A	2 rectangles, 1½" × 1¾"	2 rectangles, 2½" × 3"
	B	2 rectangles, 1" × 1¼"	2 rectangles, 1½" × 2"
	C	1 rectangle, 1" × 1½"	1 rectangle, 1½" × 2½"
	D	1 square, 1¼" × 1¼"	1 square, 2" × 2"
	E	1 rectangle, 1" × 1¾"	1 rectangle, 1½" × 3"
	F	1 rectangle, 1¾" × 2"	1 rectangle, 3" × 3½"
	G	1 rectangle, 1¼" × 1¾"	1 rectangle, 2" × 3"
	H	1 rectangle, 1½" × 2½"	1 rectangle, 2½" × 4½"
	I	1 rectangle, ¾" × 1½"	1 rectangle, 1" × 2½"
	J	1 rectangle, 1" × 3¾"	1 rectangle, 1½" × 7"
	K	1 rectangle, 2¼" × 2¾"	1 rectangle, 4" × 5"
	L	1 rectangle, 2¾" × 4¼"	1 rectangle, 5" × 8"
	M	14 squares, ¾" × ¾"	14 squares, 1" × 1"
Grass (green)	N	1 rectangle, 1" × 6½"	1 rectangle, 1½" × 12½"
Tree trunk (brown)	O	1 rectangle, 1" × 2¾"	1 rectangle, 1½" × 5"
Treetop (dark green)	P	1 rectangle, 1¾" × 3½"	1 rectangle, 3" × 6½"
	Q	1 rectangle, 1¼" × 3"	1 rectangle, 2" × 5½"
	R	1 rectangle, 1" × 2½"	1 rectangle, 1½" × 4½"
	S	1 rectangle, ¾" × 1½"	1 rectangle, 1" × 2½"
Moon (white)	T	1 square, 1½" × 1½"	1 square, 2½" × 2½"

MAKING THE BLOCK

Instructions are for both 6" and 12" blocks. Sew all pieces right sides together. When layering pieces marked with a diagonal line, stitch on the marked line. Trim the seam allowances to ¼". Press all seam allowances open to reduce bulk.

1. Draw a diagonal line on the wrong side of the M squares. Sew M to each corner of P to make the P unit.

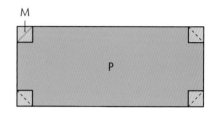

Make 1 unit.

2. Sew M squares to the top-left and top-right corners of Q, R, and S. Make one of each unit.

Make 1 of each unit.

3. Join C to S and then sew B to each end to make the S unit.

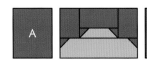

Make 1 unit.

4. Join unit S to R. Add A and F to make the R unit.

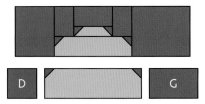

Make 1 unit.

5. Join D and G to Q. Sew unit R to Q to make the R/Q unit.

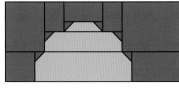

Make 1 unit.

6. Join E and A to unit P. Join the R/Q unit and the P unit to make the treetop unit.

Make 1 unit.

7. Sew M to each corner of T to make the T unit.

Make 1 unit.

8. Join I, unit T, H, and J to make the moon unit.

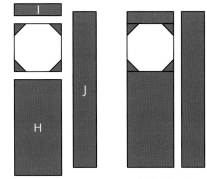

Make 1 unit.

9. Join K, O, and L. Add N to make the tree-trunk unit.

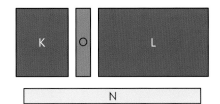

Make 1 unit.

10. Join the moon, treetop, and tree-trunk units to make the block.

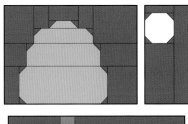

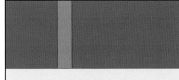

Good Night block

Campsite

FABRIC	PIECE	6" BLOCK	12" BLOCK
Sky (dark blue)	A	1 rectangle, 1¾" × 3"	1 rectangle, 3" × 5½"
	B	3 squares, 1¾" × 1¾"	3 squares, 3" × 3"
	C	1 rectangle, 1¼" × 1½"	1 rectangle, 2" × 2½"
	D	1 square, 2" × 2"	1 square, 3½" × 3½"
	E	4 squares, 1" × 1"	4 squares, 1½" × 1½"
	F	1 square, ¾" × ¾"	1 square, 1" × 1"
Left tree (light green)	G	1 square, 2½" × 2½"	1 square, 4½" × 4½"
Right tree (medium green)	H	1 rectangle, 1" × 1½"	1 rectangle, 1½" × 2½"
	I	2 rectangles, 1½" × 2"	2 rectangles, 2½" × 3½"
	J	1 square, ¾" × ¾"	1 square, 1" × 1"
	K	1 square, 1½" × 1½"	1 square, 2½" × 2½"
Middle tree (dark green)	L	1 square, ¾" × ¾"	1 square, 1" × 1"
	M	1 rectangle, 2½" × 3"	1 rectangle, 4½" × 5½"
	N	2 squares, 1¼" × 1¼"	2 squares, 2" × 2"
	O	1 square, 1½" × 1½"	1 square, 2½" × 2½"
	P	1 rectangle, ¾" × 2½"	1 rectangle, 1" × 4½"
	Q	1 rectangle, 1¾" × 3"	1 rectangle, 3" × 5½"
Grass (green dot)	R	1 rectangle, 1¼" × 6½"	1 rectangle, 2" × 12½"
Outside tent (tan)	S	2 squares, 2½" × 2½"	2 squares, 4½" × 4½"
	T	2 rectangles, 1¾" × 2½"	2 rectangles, 3" × 4½"
Inside tent (dark brown)	U	2 squares, 1¼" × 1¼"	2 squares, 2" × 2"
	V	1 rectangle, 2" × 2½"	1 rectangle, 3½" × 4½"
Firewood (brown solid)	W	1 rectangle, ¾" × 2¼"	1 rectangle, 1" × 4"
Fire (yellow)	X	1 rectangle, 1" × 1½"	1 rectangle, 1½" × 2½"
Fire (orange)	Y	1 rectangle, ¾" × 2¼"	1 rectangle, 1" × 4"
	Z	1 rectangle, 1¼" × 1½"	1 rectangle, 2" × 2½"
	AA	1 rectangle, 1" × 1½"	1 rectangle, 1½" × 2½"
	BB	1 rectangle, 1" × 2¼"	1 rectangle, 1½" × 4"
	CC	4 squares, ¾" × ¾"	4 squares, 1" × 1"

MAKING THE BLOCK

Instructions are for both 6" and 12" blocks. Sew all pieces right sides together. When layering pieces marked with a diagonal line, stitch on the marked line. Trim the seam allowances to ¼". Press all seam allowances open to reduce bulk.

1. Draw a diagonal line on the wrong side of the E squares. Sew E to the left and right ends of H to make the H unit.

Make 1 unit.

2. Draw a diagonal line on the wrong side of the B squares. Sew B to the left and right ends of Q to make the Q unit.

 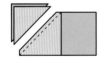

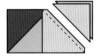

Make 1 unit.

3. Join A, C, unit Q, and unit H to make the treetop unit.

Make 1 unit.

4. Draw a diagonal line on the wrong side of the D, S, and U squares. Sew D to the top-right corner of G. Sew S on top of G. Sew E to the top-left corner of G and U to the bottom-right corner of S to make the G unit.

Make 1 unit.

5. Draw a diagonal line on the wrong side of the F square. Sew F to the top-right corner and B to the top-left corner of M. Sew S and then U to the bottom-left corner of M to make the M unit.

 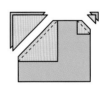

Make 1 unit.

6. Join the G and M units to make the tent-top unit.

Make 1 unit.

7. Sew E to the top-left corner of I. Draw a diagonal line on the wrong side of the N squares. Sew N to the bottom-left corner of I.

Make 1 unit.

8. Draw a diagonal line on the wrong side of the O square. Sew O to the left end of the remaining I.

 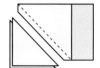

Make 1 unit.

9. Join the units from steps 7 and 8. Sew the I units to the tent-top unit to complete the unit.

Make 1 unit.

10. Sew V between two T rectangles to make the tent-bottom unit.

Make 1 unit.

11. Draw a diagonal line on the wrong side of the CC squares. Then sew CC to opposite corners of X. Repeat to sew CC to each remaining corner of X.

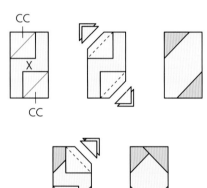

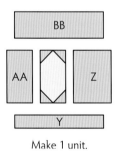

Make 1 unit.

12. Join AA, unit X, and Z. Sew BB and Y to unit X to make the flame unit.

BB

AA		Z

Y

Make 1 unit.

13. Draw a diagonal line on the wrong side of the J, K, and L squares. Sew L to the bottom-left corner and J to the bottom-right corner of the flame unit. Sew N and K to the top corners of the flame unit.

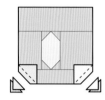

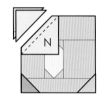
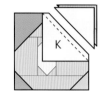

Make 1 unit.

14. Sew W and P to the flame unit to make the campfire unit.

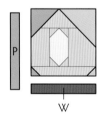

Make 1 unit.

15. Join the campfire unit, tent-bottom unit, and R to complete the tent bottom.

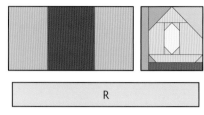

Make 1 unit.

16. Join the treetop, tent-top, and tent-bottom units to make the block.

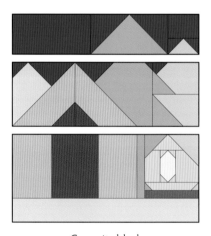

Campsite block

Grasshopper

FABRIC	PIECE	6" BLOCK	12" BLOCK
Background (white)	A	1 rectangle, 2" × 2½"	1 rectangle, 3½" × 4½"
	B	1 rectangle, 1½" × 2¼"	1 rectangle, 2½" × 4"
	C	1 rectangle, 2½" × 3¼"	1 rectangle, 4½" × 6"
	D	2 squares, 2" × 2"	2 squares, 3½" × 3½"
	E	5 squares, 1" × 1"	5 squares, 1½" × 1½"
	F	4 squares, 1¼" × 1¼"	4 squares, 2" × 2"
	G	1 rectangle, 2¼" × 5"	1 rectangle, 4" × 9½"
	H	1 rectangle, 1" × 1½"	1 rectangle, 1½" × 2½"
	I	1 rectangle, ¾" × 1"	1 rectangle, 1" × 1½"
	J	1 rectangle, 1" × 2¼"	1 rectangle, 1½" × 4"
	K	1 rectangle, ¾" × 1½"	1 rectangle, 1" × 2½"
	L	1 rectangle, ¾" × 2"	1 rectangle, 1" × 3½"
	M	1 square, 1½" × 1½"	1 square, 2½" × 2½"
Grasshopper body (light green)	N	1 rectangle, 1¾" × 2"	1 rectangle, 3" × 3½"
	O	1 rectangle, 2¼" × 2½"	1 rectangle, 4" × 4½"
	P	1 rectangle, 1½" × 1¾"	1 rectangle, 2½" × 3"
	Q	1 square, 1¼" × 1¼"	1 square, 2" × 2"
	R	1 rectangle, 1¼" × 1½"	1 rectangle, 2" × 2½"
	S	1 rectangle, 1¼" × 2"	1 rectangle, 2" × 3½"
Wing (light blue)	T	1 rectangle, 2" × 2¼"	1 rectangle, 3½" × 4"
Legs (dark green)	U	2 squares, 1½" × 1½"	2 squares, 2½" × 2½"
	V	1 rectangle, 1" × 1¼"	1 rectangle, 1½" × 2"
	W	1 rectangle, ¾" × 2¼"	1 rectangle, 1" × 4"
	X	2 squares, ¾" × ¾"	2 squares, 1" × 1"
	Y	1 square, 1¼" × 1¼"	1 square, 2" × 2"

MAKING THE BLOCK

Instructions are for both 6" and 12" blocks. Sew all pieces right sides together. When layering pieces marked with a diagonal line, stitch on the marked line. Trim the seam allowances to ¼". Press all seam allowances open to reduce bulk.

1. Draw a diagonal line on the wrong side of the E squares. Sew E to the bottom-left and bottom-right corners of N to make the N unit.

Make 1 unit.

2. Sew L and A to unit N to make the head unit.

Make 1 unit.

3. Draw a diagonal line on the wrong side of the F and M squares. Sew F to the bottom-right corner of U. Sew M to U to make the U unit.

Make 1 unit.

4. Sew H and D to unit U to make the front-leg unit.

Make 1 unit.

5. Join the head and front-leg units to make the front section.

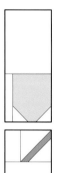 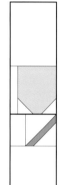

Make 1 section.

6. Draw a diagonal line on the wrong side of the remaining D square. Sew D to the left end of T. Sew B to unit T to make the wing unit.

 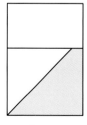

Make 1 unit.

7. Sew E to the right end of V to make the V unit.

Make 1 unit.

8. Sew I and J to unit V. Add C to make the C unit.

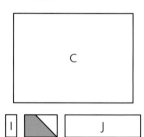

Make 1 unit.

9. Join the wing unit to unit C to make the wing section.

Make 1 section.

10. Sew F to the bottom-left corner of O to make the O unit.

Make 1 unit.

11. Draw a diagonal line on the wrong side of Q and the remaining U. Sew U to the right end of P. Sew Q to the top-right corner of U to make the P unit.

Make 1 unit.

12. Draw a diagonal line on the wrong side of the X squares. Sew X to the bottom-left corner of R and sew E to the bottom-right corner of R to make the R unit.

Make 1 unit.

13. Join the P and R units. Add K to make the P/R unit.

Make 1 unit.

14. Sew F to the right end of S. Sew X to the top-right corner of S to make the S unit.

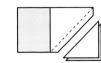

Make 1 unit.

15. Sew F to Y. Sew E to the bottom-left corner of Y to make the Y unit.

Make 1 unit.

16. Join the S and Y units. Sew the S/Y unit to the P/R unit to make the back-leg unit.

Make 1 unit.

17. Join the O unit and W to the back-leg unit to make the body section.

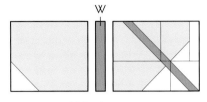

Make 1 section.

18. Join the wing section, body section, and G. Add the front section to make the block.

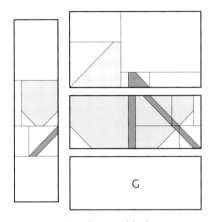

Grasshopper block

Dragonfly

FABRIC	PIECE	6" BLOCK	12" BLOCK
Background (white)	A	1 rectangle, 1" × 6½"	1 rectangle, 1½" × 12½"
	B	2 rectangles, 1" × 3¼"	2 rectangles, 1½" × 6"
	C	2 rectangles, ¾" × 3"	2 rectangles, 1" × 5½"
	D	2 rectangles, ¾" × 5½"	2 rectangles, 1" × 10½"
	E	8 squares, 1" × 1"	8 squares, 1½" × 1½"
	F	10 squares, ¾" × ¾"	10 squares, 1" × 1"
	G	2 rectangles, 3" × 3¾"	2 rectangles, 5½" × 7"
Wings (pink)	H	4 rectangles, 1¼" × 3"	4 rectangles, 2" × 5½"
Body and head (blue)	I	1 rectangle, 1" × 5½"	1 rectangle, 1½" × 10½"
	J	1 square, 1" × 1"	1 square, 1½" × 1½"

MAKING THE BLOCK

Instructions are for both 6" and 12" blocks. Sew all pieces right sides together. When layering pieces marked with a diagonal line, stitch on the marked line. Trim the seam allowances to ¼". Press all seam allowances open to reduce bulk.

1. Draw a diagonal line on the wrong side of the E squares. Sew E to the bottom-left and bottom-right corners of H. Make four H units.

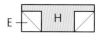

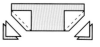

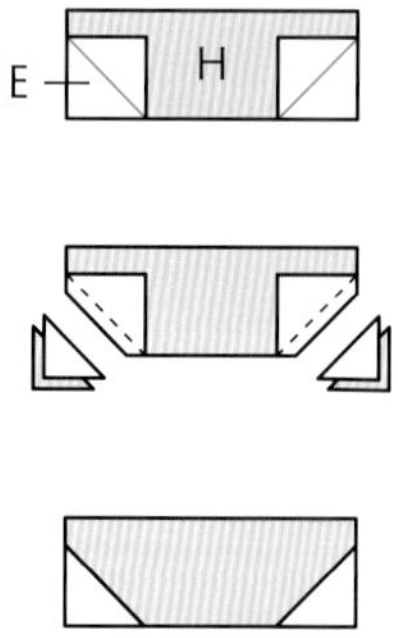

Make 4 units.

2. Draw a diagonal line on the wrong side of the F squares. Sew F to the top-left corner of two H units. Sew F to the top-right corner of two H units. Make two left and two right wing units.

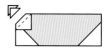

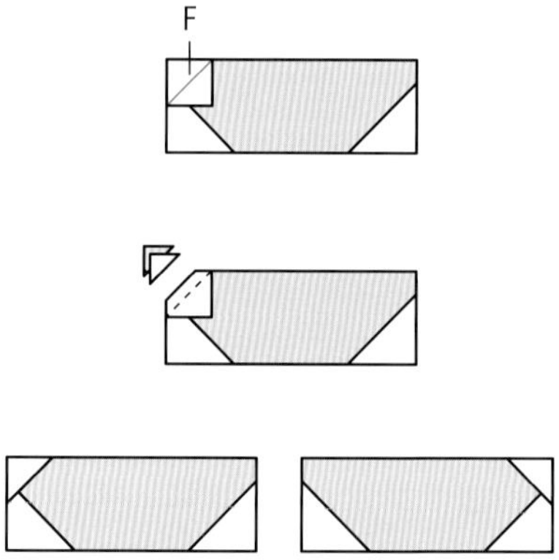

Make 2 of each unit.

3. Join two matching wing units, one C, and one G. Make one left wing and one right wing section.

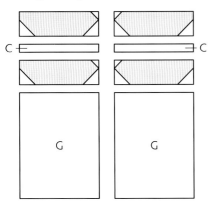

Make 1 of each section.

4. Sew F to the corners of I to make the I unit.

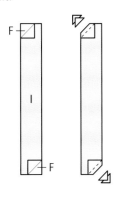

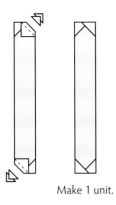

Make 1 unit.

5. Join two D rectangles, the wing sections, and the I unit to make the body unit.

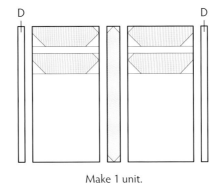

Make 1 unit.

6. Sew F to the bottom-left and bottom-right corners of J. Sew the J unit between two B rectangles to make the head unit.

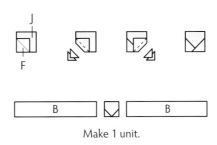

Make 1 unit.

7. Join A, the head unit, and the body unit to make the block.

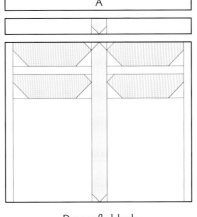

Dragonfly block

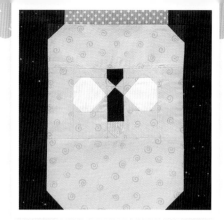

Lightning Bug

FABRIC	PIECE	6" BLOCK	12" BLOCK
Background (navy)	A	2 rectangles, 1" × 2"	2 rectangles, 1½" × 3½"
	B	2 rectangles, 1½" × 6"	2 rectangles, 2½" × 11½"
	C	2 squares, 1" × 1"	2 squares, 1½" × 1½"
	D	2 squares, 1¼" × 1¼"	2 squares, 2" × 2"
Lid (light gray)	E	1 rectangle, 1" × 3½"	1 rectangle, 1½" × 6½"
Jar (light blue)	F	1 rectangle, 1¾" × 4½"	1 rectangle, 3" × 8½"
	G	2 rectangles, 1¼" × 2½"	2 rectangles, 2" × 4½"
	H	1 rectangle, 2¾" × 4½"	1 rectangle, 5" × 8½"
	I	2 rectangles, ¾" × 1½"	2 rectangles, 1" × 2½"
	J	2 rectangles, 1¼" × 1½"	2 rectangles, 2" × 2½"
	K	4 squares, 1" × 1"	4 squares, 1½" × 1½"
	L	10 squares, ¾" × ¾"	10 squares, 1" × 1"
Light (yellow)	M	1 square, 1" × 1"	1 square, 1½" × 1½"
Lightning bug (black)	N	1 rectangle, 1" × 1½"	1 rectangle, 1½" × 2½"
	O	1 square, 1" × 1"	1 square, 1½" × 1½"
Wings (white)	P	2 squares, 1½" × 1½"	2 squares, 2½" × 2½"

MAKING THE BLOCK

Instructions are for both 6" and 12" blocks. Sew all pieces right sides together. When layering pieces marked with a diagonal line, stitch on the marked line. Trim the seam allowances to ¼". Press all seam allowances open to reduce bulk.

1. Draw a diagonal line on the wrong side of the C squares. Sew C to the top-left and top-right corners of F to make the F unit.

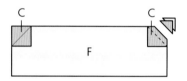

Make 1 unit.

2. Draw a diagonal line on the wrong side of the D squares. Sew D to the bottom-left and bottom-right corners of H to make the H unit.

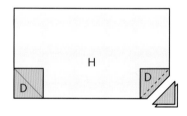

Make 1 unit.

3. Sew E between two A rectangles to make the lid unit.

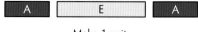

Make 1 unit.

4. Draw a diagonal line on the wrong side of the L squares. Sew L to the bottom-left and bottom-right corners of O to make the O unit. Sew L to the bottom-left and bottom-right corners of M to make one M unit.

Make 1 of each unit.

5. Sew L to the top-left and top-right corners of N to make one N unit.

Make 1 unit.

6. Join the O, N, and M units to make the body unit.

Make 1 unit.

7. Draw a diagonal line on the wrong side of the K squares. Sew L to the top-left and K to the bottom-right corners of P. Sew L to the bottom-left and K to the top-right corners to make a wing unit. Make two units.

Make 2 units.

8. Join I and J to each wing unit. Make one of each section.

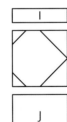 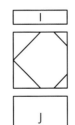

Make 1 of each section.

9. Join two G rectangles, the wing sections, and the body unit to make the lightning bug unit.

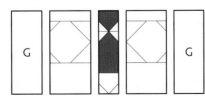

Make 1 unit.

10. Join the F and H units to the lightning bug unit to make the jar unit.

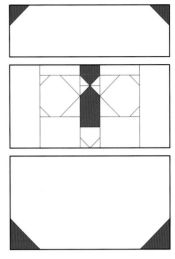

Make 1 unit.

11. Join two B rectangles and the jar unit. Add the lid unit to make the block.

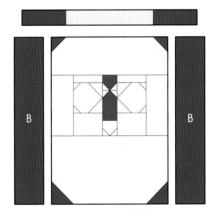

Lightning Bug block

Butterfly

FABRIC	PIECE	6" BLOCK	12" BLOCK
Background (white)	A	2 rectangles, ¾" × 3¼"	2 rectangles, 1" × 6"
	B	1 square, 1" × 1"	1 square, 1½" × 1½"
	C	6 squares, 1¼" × 1¼"	6 squares, 2" × 2"
	D	2 squares, 1½" × 1½"	2 squares, 2½" × 2½"
	E	2 rectangles, 1½" × 2"	2 rectangles, 2½" × 3½"
	F	16 squares, ¾" × ¾"	16 squares, 1" × 1"
	G	2 rectangles, ¾" × 1"	2 rectangles, 1" × 1½"
	H	2 rectangles, ¾" × 1¾"	2 rectangles, 1" × 3"
	I	2 rectangles, 1" × 1¼"	2 rectangles, 1½" × 2"
Wings (yellow)	J	2 rectangles, 3¼" × 4¼"	2 rectangles, 6" × 8"
	K	2 rectangles, 2" × 2¼"	2 rectangles, 3½" × 4"
	L	2 rectangles, ¾" × 1¾"	2 rectangles, 1" × 3"
	M	2 squares, 1" × 1"	2 squares, 1½" × 1½"
Body (blue)	N	1 rectangle, 1" × 5½"	1 rectangle, 1½" × 10½"
	O	1 square, 1" × 1"	1 square, 1½" × 1½"

MAKING THE BLOCK

Instructions are for both 6" and 12" blocks. Sew all pieces right sides together. When layering pieces marked with a diagonal line, stitch on the marked line. Trim the seam allowances to ¼". Press all seam allowances open to reduce bulk.

1. Draw a diagonal line on the wrong side of the C and D squares. Sew D to the top-right corner of J. Sew C to the top-left and bottom-left corners of J. Sew A to J to make the top-left wing. Repeat to make the top-right wing, making sure to reverse the position of the C and D squares.

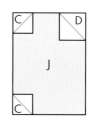
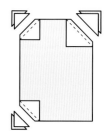

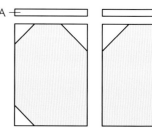

Make 1 of each unit.

2. Draw a diagonal line on the wrong side of the F squares. Sew C to the top-left corner and sew F to the bottom-right corner of K. Make one K unit and one reversed.

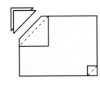

Make 1 of each unit.

3. Sew E to each K unit to make the middle-wing units. Make one of each unit.

Make 1 of each unit.

4. Sew F to the right end of L to make an L unit. Sew H to unit L. Sew G to the unit to make a bottom-wing section. Make one and one reversed.

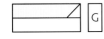

Make 1 of each section.

5. Sew F to the top-left corner of M. Sew F to the bottom-left and bottom-right corners of M. Make two M units.

Make 2 units.

6. Join an I, an M unit, and a bottom-wing section. Make one of each bottom-wing unit.

Make 1 of each unit.

7. Join the top, middle, and bottom-wing units to make the left wing. Repeat to make the right wing.

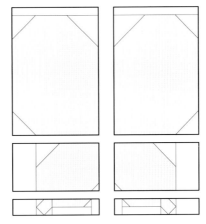

Make 1 of each unit.

8. Sew F to the corners of N to make the N unit.

Make 1 unit.

9. Sew F to the bottom-left and bottom-right corners of O to make the O unit.

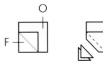

Make 1 unit.

10. Join B, unit O, and unit N to make the body unit.

Make 1 unit.

11. Join the left and right wing units to the body unit to make the block.

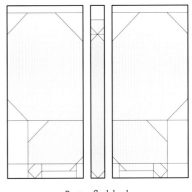

Butterfly block

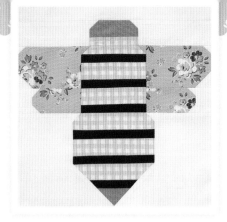

Bee

FABRIC	PIECE	6" BLOCK	12" BLOCK
Background (white)	A	1 rectangle, 1" × 6½"	1 rectangle, 1½" × 12½"
	B	2 rectangles, 1¼" × 2¾"	2 rectangles, 2" × 5"
	C	10 squares, ¾" × ¾"	10 squares, 1" × 1"
	D	2 squares, 1" × 1"	2 squares, 1½" × 1½"
	E	2 rectangles, 1" × 1¼"	2 rectangles, 1½" × 2"
	F	2 rectangles, 2¼" × 3¼"	2 rectangles, 4" × 6"
	G	2 squares, 1¾" × 1¾"	2 squares, 3" × 3"
Head and stinger (gray)	H	1 rectangle, 1" × 2"	1 rectangle, 1½" × 3½"
	I	1 rectangle, 1" × 3"	1 rectangle, 1½" × 5½"
Wings (light blue)	J	2 rectangles, 1¾" × 2½"	2 rectangles, 3" × 4½"
	K	2 rectangles, 1¼" × 2"	2 rectangles, 2" × 3½"
	L	2 squares, ¾" × ¾"	2 squares, 1" × 1"
Stripes (yellow)	M	1 rectangle, ¾" × 2"	1 rectangle, 1" × 3½"
	N	1 rectangle, ¾" × 2½"	1 rectangle, 1" × 4½"
	O	2 rectangles, 1" × 2½"	2 rectangles, 1½" × 4½"
	P	3 rectangles, 1" × 3"	3 rectangles, 1½" × 5½"
Stripes (black)	Q	3 rectangles, ¾" × 2½"	3 rectangles, 1" × 4½"
	R	3 rectangles, ¾" × 3"	3 rectangles, 1" × 5½"

MAKING THE BLOCK

Instructions are for both 6" and 12" blocks. Sew all pieces right sides together. When layering pieces marked with a diagonal line, stitch on the marked line. Trim the seam allowances to ¼". Press all seam allowances open to reduce bulk.

1. Draw a diagonal line on the wrong side of the C squares. Sew C to the top-left and top-right corners of H. Sew M to H to make the head unit.

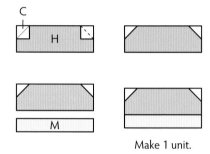

Make 1 unit.

2. Sew the head unit between the B rectangles. Sew A to the unit to make the head section.

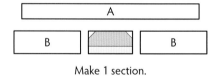

Make 1 section.

3. Join N, Q, and O to make the middle body. Draw a diagonal line on the wrong side of the L squares. Sew L to the top-left and top-right corners of the middle body.

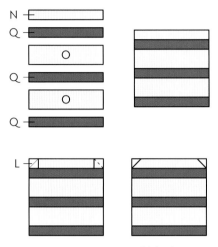

Make 1 unit.

4. Draw a diagonal line on the wrong side of the D squares. Sew D to the top-left corner and C to the bottom-left corner of J. Make one J unit and one reversed for the left and right wings.

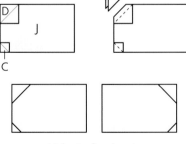

Make 1 of each unit.

5. Sew C to the top-left and bottom-left corners of K. Make two units. Sew E to each unit to make two K units.

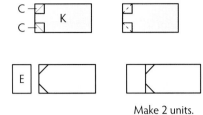

Make 2 units.

6. Sew a K unit to the left and right wings to make one of each wing unit.

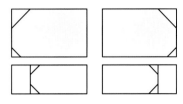

Make 1 of each unit.

7. Join the left and right wings to the middle body to make the middle-bee section.

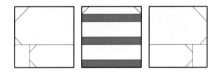

Make 1 section.

8. Join P, R, and I rectangles to make the bottom body.

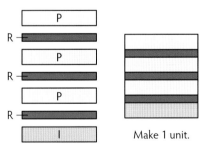

Make 1 unit.

9. Sew C to the top-left and top-right corners of the bottom body. Draw a diagonal line on the wrong

side of the G squares. Sew G to the bottom-left and bottom-right corners of the bottom body.

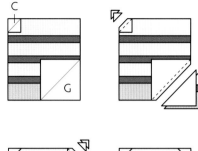

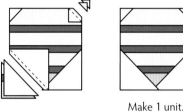

Make 1 unit.

10. Sew the bottom body between two F rectangles to make the bottom-bee section.

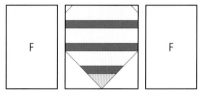

Make 1 section.

11. Join the head, middle-bee, and bottom-bee sections to make the block.

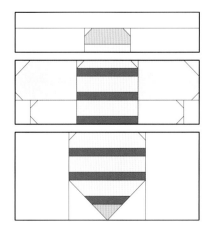

Bee block

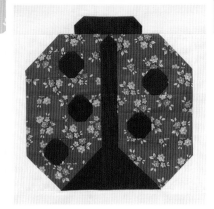

Ladybug

FABRIC	PIECE	6" BLOCK	12" BLOCK
Background (white)	A	2 rectangles, 1½" × 2½"	2 rectangles, 2½" × 4½"
	B	1 rectangle, 1" × 2½"	1 rectangle, 1½" × 4½"
	C	2 squares, ¾" × ¾"	2 squares, 1" × 1"
	D	4 squares, 1½" × 1½"	4 squares, 2½" × 2½"
	E	2 rectangles, 1" × 5"	2 rectangles, 1½" × 9½"
	F	1 rectangle, 1" × 6½"	1 rectangle, 1½" × 12½"
Head and body (black)	G	1 rectangle, 1" × 2½"	1 rectangle, 1½" × 4½"
	H	2 squares, 1¾" × 1¾"	2 squares, 3" × 3"
	I	1 rectangle, 1" × 5"	1 rectangle, 1½" × 9½"
Ladybug spots (black)	J	5 squares, 1¼" × 1¼"	5 squares, 2" × 2"
Wings (red)	K	4 rectangles, 1" × 2¾"	4 rectangles, 1½" × 5"
	L	2 rectangles, 1¼" × 1½"	2 rectangles, 2" × 2½"
	M	2 rectangles, 1" × 1¼"	2 rectangles, 1½" × 2"
	N	2 rectangles, ¾" × 1¼"	2 rectangles, 1" × 2"
	O	1 rectangle, 1¼" × 2¾"	1 rectangle, 2" × 5"
	P	1 rectangle, 1½" × 2¾"	1 rectangle, 2½" × 5"
	Q	2 squares, 1¼" × 1¼"	2 squares, 2" × 2"
	R	1 rectangle, 2" × 2¾"	1 rectangle, 3½" × 5"
	S	22 squares, ¾" × ¾"	22 squares, 1" × 1"
	T	2 rectangles, 1¼" × 1¾"	2 rectangles, 2" × 3"

MAKING THE BLOCK

Instructions are for both 6" and 12" blocks. Sew all pieces right sides together. When layering pieces marked with a diagonal line, stitch on the marked line. Trim the seam allowances to ¼". Press all seam allowances open to reduce bulk.

1. Draw a diagonal line on the wrong side of the C squares. Sew C to the top-left and top-right corners of G to make the G unit.

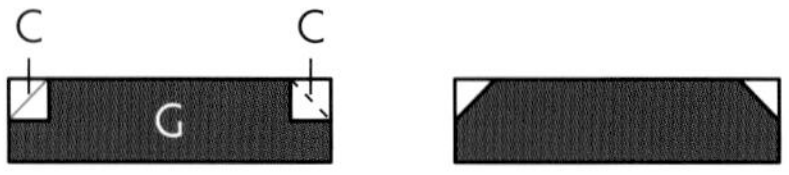

Make 1 unit.

2. Sew B to unit G. Sew A to unit G to make the head unit.

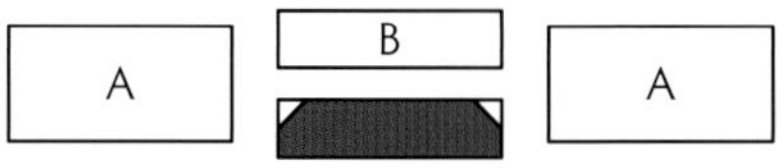

Make 1 unit.

3. Draw a diagonal line on the wrong side of the S squares. Sew S to each corner of J. Make five J units.

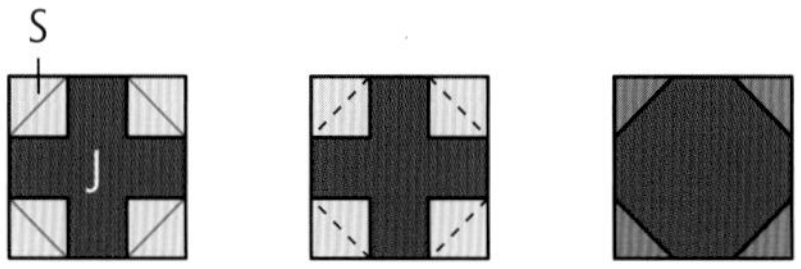

Make 5 units.

4. Join L, unit J, and M to make a spot unit. Make two units.

Make 2 units.

5. Join T, unit J, and N to make a spot unit. Make two units.

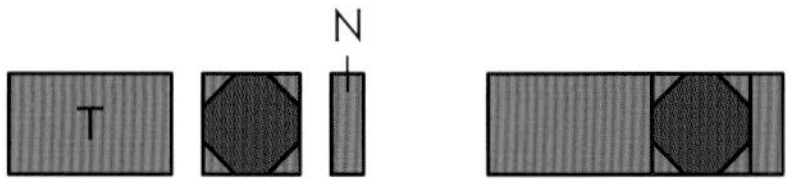

Make 2 units.

6. Join three K rectangles, O, the spot units from step 4, and one spot unit from step 5 for the left wing.

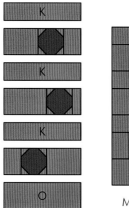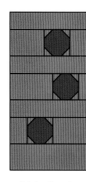

Make 1 unit.

7. Join a J unit between two Q squares to make a spot unit.

Make 1 unit.

8. Join P, K, R, the remaining spot unit from step 5, and the spot unit from step 7 to make the right wing.

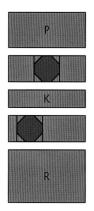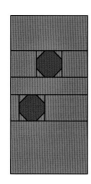

Make 1 unit.

9. Draw a diagonal line on the wrong side of the D and H squares. Sew D to the top-left and bottom-left corners of the left wing. Sew H to the bottom-right corner of the left wing.

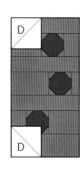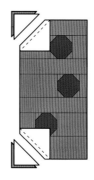

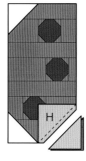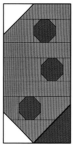

Make 1 unit.

10. Sew D to the top-right and bottom-right corners of the right wing. Sew H to the bottom-left corner of the right wing.

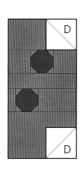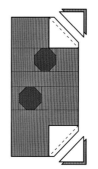

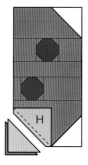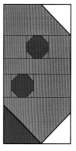

Make 1 unit.

11. Sew S to the top-left and top-right corners of I to make an I unit.

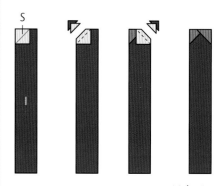

Make 1 unit.

12. Join the left and right wings to the I unit. Add E to make the body unit.

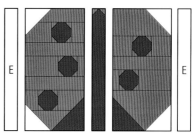

Make 1 unit.

13. Join the head unit, body unit, and F to make the block.

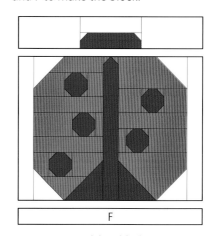

Ladybug block

Coneflower

FABRIC	PIECE	6" BLOCK	12" BLOCK
Background (white)	A	1 rectangle, 1" × 6½"	1 rectangle, 1½" × 12½"
	B	2 rectangles, 1½" × 2½"	2 rectangles, 2½" × 4½"
	C	8 squares, 1" × 1"	8 squares, 1½" × 1½"
	D	2 squares, 2" × 2"	2 squares, 3½" × 3½"
	E	2 rectangles, 1" × 4"	2 rectangles, 1½" × 7½"
	F	2 rectangles, ¾" × 1"	2 rectangles, 1" × 1½"
	G	2 rectangles, 1½" × 3¼"	2 rectangles, 2½" × 6"
Flower center (brown)	H	1 rectangle, 1½" × 2½"	1 rectangle, 2½" × 4½"
Light petals (light purple)	I	1 rectangle, 1½" × 4"	1 rectangle, 2½" × 7½"
	J	1 rectangle, 2" × 3½"	1 rectangle, 3½" × 6½"
	K	1 rectangle, 1" × 1½"	1 rectangle, 1½" × 2½"
	L	1 square, 1" × 1"	1 square, 1½" × 1½"
Dark petals (dark purple)	M	1 rectangle, 2" × 3½"	1 rectangle, 3½" × 6½"
	N	1 rectangle, 1½" × 4"	1 rectangle, 2½" × 7½"
	O	1 rectangle, 1" × 1½"	1 rectangle, 1½" × 2½"
	P	1 square, 1" × 1"	1 square, 1½" × 1½"
Stem (green)	Q	1 square, 1" × 1"	1 square, 1½" × 1½"
	R	1 rectangle, 1" × 1½"	1 rectangle, 1½" × 2½"

MAKING THE BLOCK

Instructions are for both 6" and 12" blocks. Sew all pieces right sides together. When layering pieces marked with a diagonal line, stitch on the marked line. Trim the seam allowances to ¼". Press all seam allowances open to reduce bulk.

1. Draw a diagonal line on the wrong side of the C squares. Stitch C to the top-left and top-right corners of H. Sew H between the B rectangles to make the flower-center section.

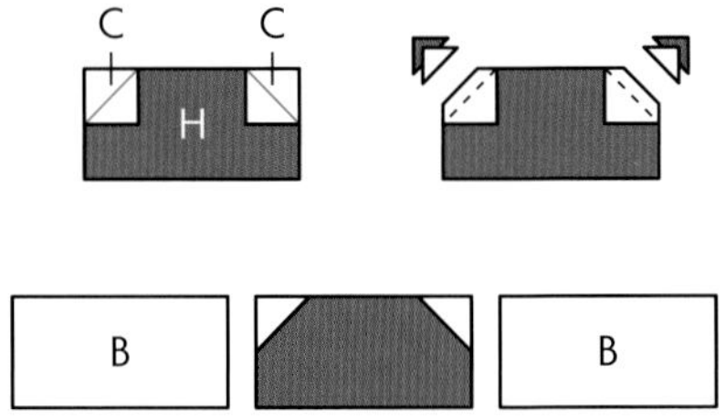

Make 1 section.

2. Sew Q between the F rectangles. Draw a diagonal line on the wrong side of the L and P squares. Stitch P to the left end and sew L to the right end of the unit to make the top-stem unit.

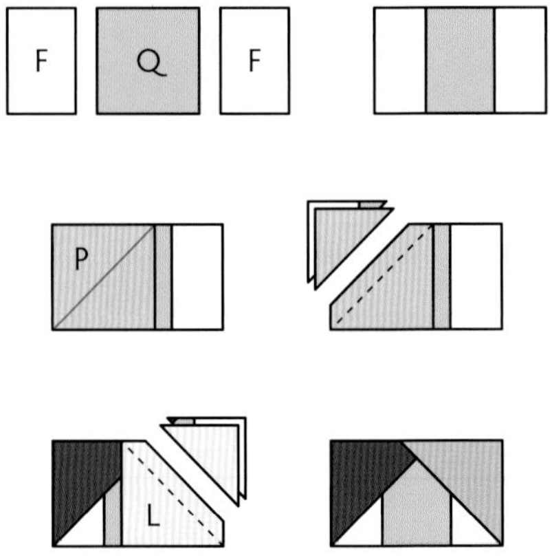

Make 1 unit.

3. Sew C to the left end of O. Sew C to the right end of K. Make one of each unit.

Make 1 of each unit.

4. Join O and K units to the top-stem unit to make the top-stem section.

Make 1 section.

5. Join M and J. Sew the unit to the top-stem section to make the middle-petal section.

Make 1 section.

6. Sew C to the bottom-left and bottom-right corners of I. Sew C to the bottom-left and bottom-right corners of N.

 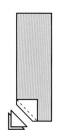 

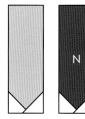

Make 1 of each unit.

7. Join the I and N units to the middle-petal section to make the flower unit.

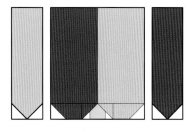

Make 1 unit.

8. Draw a diagonal line on the wrong side of the D squares. Sew D to the top-left and top-right corners of the flower unit. Sew E rectangles to the flower unit to make the flower section.

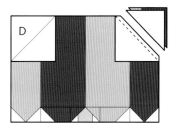

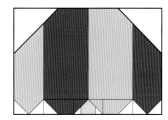

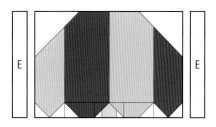

Make 1 section.

9. Sew R between the G rectangles to make the bottom-stem section.

Make 1 section.

10. Join the flower-center, flower, and bottom-stem sections. Add A to make the block.

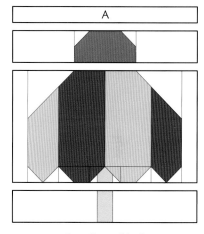

Coneflower block

Watering Can

FABRIC	PIECE	6" BLOCK	12" BLOCK
Background (white)	A	1 rectangle, 2¼" × 3"	1 rectangle, 4" × 5½"
	B	2 rectangles, 1¾" × 2¼"	2 rectangles, 3" × 4"
	C	1 rectangle, 1¼" × 2¾"	1 rectangle, 2" × 5"
	D	2 rectangles, 1¼" × 2¼"	2 rectangles, 2" × 4"
	E	4 squares, ¾" × ¾"	4 squares, 1" × 1"
	F	1 rectangle, 1½" × 2"	1 rectangle, 2½" × 3½"
	G	1 rectangle, 1¾" × 3"	1 rectangle, 3" × 5½"
	H	4 squares, 1½" × 1½"	4 squares, 2½" × 2½"
	I	1 rectangle, 1" × 1½"	1 rectangle, 1½" × 2½"
Handles and spout (navy)	J	2 rectangles, ¾" × 2¾"	2 rectangles, 1" × 5"
	K	1 square, 1¾" × 1¾"	1 square, 3" × 3"
	L	4 rectangles, ¾" × 1¼"	4 rectangles, 1" × 2"
Watering can (light blue)	M	1 square, 1¼" × 1¼"	1 square, 2" × 2"
	N	1 square, 1" × 1"	1 square, 1½" × 1½"
	O	1 rectangle, 3¼" × 4¾"	1 rectangle, 6" × 9"
	P	1 rectangle, 1½" × 2¾"	1 rectangle, 2½" × 5"

MAKING THE BLOCK

Instructions are for both 6" and 12" blocks. Sew all pieces right sides together. When layering pieces marked with a diagonal line, stitch on the marked line. Trim the seam allowances to ¼". Press all seam allowances open to reduce bulk.

1. Sew L rectangles to the ends of D. Make two D units.

Make 2 units.

2. Draw a diagonal line on the wrong side of the E squares. Sew E to each end of J. Join J and D units to make a handle unit. Make two units.

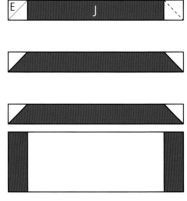

Make 2 units.

3. Join C to a handle unit. Sew A and B to the unit to make the top-handle section.

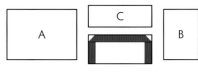

Make 1 section.

4. Join I and F to the remaining handle unit to make the side-handle section.

Make 1 section.

5. Draw a diagonal line on the wrong side of the K and M squares. Sew K to the end of B. Sew M to the bottom-right corner of K to make the B unit.

Make 1 unit.

6. Draw a diagonal line on the wrong side of the N square. Sew N to the top-right corner of G to make the G unit.

Make 1 unit.

7. Join B and G units to make the spout unit.

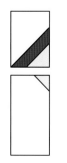 

Make 1 unit.

8. Draw a diagonal line on the wrong side of two H squares. Sew H to each end of P to make the P unit, making sure the lines are going in the same direction.

 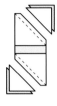

Make 1 unit.

9. Sew H to unit P to make the spout-neck unit. Join the unit to the spout unit to make the spout section.

 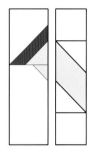

Make 1 section.

10. Join the spout section, O, and the side-handle section. Add the top-handle section to make the block.

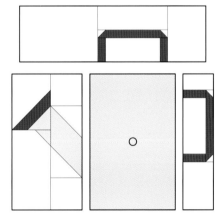

Watering Can block

Pansy

FABRIC	PIECE	6" BLOCK	12" BLOCK
Background (white)	A	2 rectangles, 1¼" × 6½"	2 rectangles, 2" × 12½"
	B	2 rectangles, 1" × 2"	2 rectangles, 1½" × 3½"
	C	2 rectangles, 1" × 1½"	2 rectangles, 1½" × 2½"
	D	3 squares, 1½" × 1½"	3 squares, 2½" × 2½"
	E	12 squares, 1" × 1"	12 squares, 1½" × 1½"
	F	1 rectangle, 1½" × 2½"	1 rectangle, 2½" × 4½"
Top petals (dark purple)	G	2 rectangles, 2" × 3"	2 rectangles, 3½" × 5½"
	H	2 rectangles, 1" × 1½"	2 rectangles, 1½" × 2½"
	I	4 squares, 1" × 1"	4 squares, 1½" × 1½"
Front petals (light purple)	J	4 rectangles, 2" × 2½"	4 rectangles, 3½" × 4½"
Flower center (yellow)	K	4 squares, 1" × 1"	4 squares, 1½" × 1½"
Leaf (green)	L	1 square, 1½" × 1½"	1 square, 2½" × 2½"
	M	2 squares, 1" × 1"	2 squares, 1½" × 1½"

MAKING THE BLOCK

Instructions are for both 6" and 12" blocks. Sew all pieces right sides together. When layering pieces marked with a diagonal line, stitch on the marked line. Trim the seam allowances to ¼". Press all seam allowances open to reduce bulk.

1. Draw a diagonal line on the wrong side of two D and the E squares. Sew D to the top-left corner and E to the top-right corner of G. Sew D and E to the top corners of a second G, making sure to reverse the position of the D and E squares. Join the G units, matching the E triangles. Sew B to the unit to make the top-petal section.

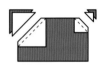

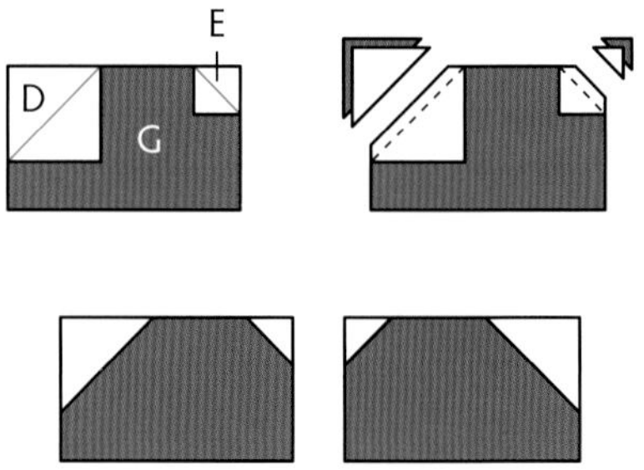

Make 1 of each unit.

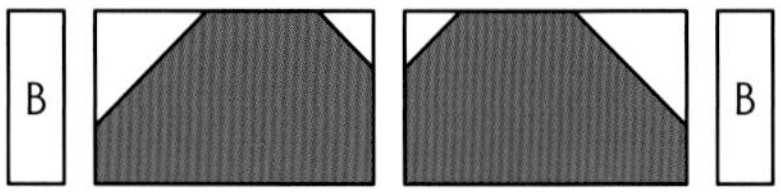

Make 1 section.

2. Draw a diagonal line on the wrong side of the I, K, and M squares. Sew I to the top-left and top-right corners of J. Make two units.

Make 2 units.

3. Sew M to the bottom-left and K to the bottom-right corners of one J unit. Sew K to the bottom-left and E to the bottom-right corners of the other J unit. Join the J units, matching the K triangles, to make the middle-petal unit.

Make 1 unit.

Make 1 unit.

Make 1 unit.

4. Sew E to the bottom-left and bottom-right corners of J. Make two units.

Make 2 units.

5. Sew M to the top-left corner and sew K to the top-right corner of one J unit. Sew K to the top-left corner and E to the top-right corner of the remaining J unit. Join the J units, matching the K triangles, to make the bottom-petal unit.

Make 1 unit.

Make 1 unit.

Make 1 unit.

6. Sew E to one end of H. Repeat to make a reversed H unit.

Make 1 of each unit.

7. Sew E to the top-left and bottom-left corners of L to make the L unit.

Make 1 unit.

8. Join D, unit L, unit H, and C to make the left-flower unit.

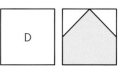

Make 1 unit.

9. Join F, the reversed H unit, and C to make the right-flower unit.

Make 1 unit.

10. Join the middle- and bottom-petal units. Add the left- and right-flower units to make the flower section.

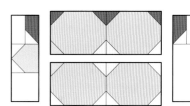

Make 1 section.

11. Join the A rectangles, top-petal section, and flower section to make the block.

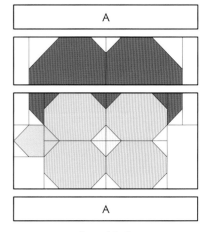

Pansy block

Tulip

FABRIC	PIECE	6" BLOCK	12" BLOCK
Background (white)	A	2 rectangles, 1¾" × 3"	2 rectangles, 3" × 5½"
	B	2 rectangles, 1½" × 2¼"	2 rectangles, 2½" × 4"
	C	2 squares, 1" × 1"	2 squares, 1½" × 1½"
	D	2 rectangles, 1½" × 4"	2 rectangles, 2½" × 7½"
	E	2 rectangles, 1" × 2¼"	2 rectangles, 1½" × 4"
	F	2 squares, 2¼" × 2¼"	2 squares, 4" × 4"
	G	2 squares, 1¾" × 1¾"	2 squares, 3" × 3"
Stem and leaves (green)	H	1 rectangle, 1" × 4"	1 rectangle, 1½" × 7½"
	I	2 rectangles, 2¼" × 3½"	2 rectangles, 4" × 6½"
Outer petals (dark pink)	J	2 rectangles, 2" × 2¼"	2 rectangles, 3½" × 4"
	K	2 squares, 1½" × 1½"	2 squares, 2½" × 2½"
Inner petal (light pink)	L	4 squares, 1¼" × 1¼"	4 squares, 2" × 2"

MAKING THE BLOCK

Instructions are for both 6" and 12" blocks. Sew all pieces right sides together. When layering pieces marked with a diagonal line, stitch on the marked line. Trim the seam allowances to ¼". Press all seam allowances open to reduce bulk.

1. Draw a diagonal line on the wrong side of the K and L squares. Sew K to the left end and sew L to the right end of B to make a B unit. Repeat to make a reversed B unit. Join the B units, matching the L triangles, to make the top-tulip unit.

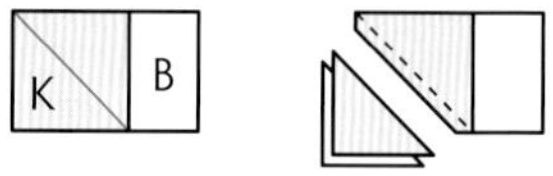

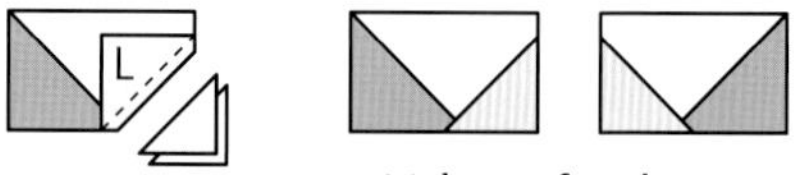

Make 1 of each unit.

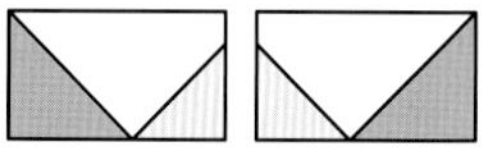

Make 1 unit.

2. Draw a diagonal line on the wrong side of the C squares. Sew L to the top-right corner and C to the bottom-left corner of J to make a J unit. Repeat to make a reversed J unit. Join the J units, matching the L triangles, to make the bottom-tulip unit.

Make 1 of each unit.

Make 1 unit.

3. Join the top- and bottom-tulip units to make the flower unit. Sew A to the flower unit to make the flower section.

 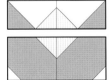

Make 1 section.

4. Draw a diagonal line on the wrong side of the F and G squares. Sew F to one end of I. Sew G to the bottom-left corner of I to make an I unit. Repeat to make a reversed I unit. Sew E to each I unit to make one of each leaf unit.

Make 1 of each unit.

5. Join the leaf units, H, and D to make the stem section.

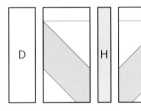

Make 1 section.

6. Join the flower and stem sections to make the block.

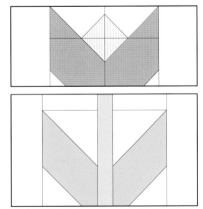

Tulip block

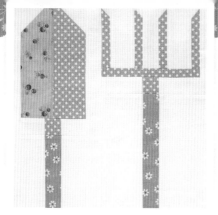

Garden Tools

FABRIC	PIECE	6" BLOCK	12" BLOCK
Background (white)	A	1 rectangle, ¾" × 6½"	1 rectangle, 1" × 12½"
	B	2 squares, 1¼" × 1¼"	2 squares, 2" × 2"
	C	2 rectangles, 1" × 1¼"	2 rectangles, 1½" × 2"
	D	2 rectangles, 1¼" × 2¾"	2 rectangles, 2" × 5"
	E	1 rectangle, 1" × 6½"	1 rectangle, 1½" × 12½"
	F	2 rectangles, 1" × 1¾"	2 rectangles, 1½" × 3"
	G	1 rectangle, 1¾" × 4"	1 rectangle, 3" × 7½"
	H	1 rectangle, 2" × 4"	1 rectangle, 3½" × 7½"
	I	2 rectangles, 1¼" × 2¼"	2 rectangles, 2" × 4"
	J	1 rectangle, ¾" × 3"	1 rectangle, 1" × 5½"
	K	4 squares, ¾" × ¾"	4 squares, 1" × 1"
	L	1 rectangle, 1" × 2¼"	1 rectangle, 1½" × 4"
Tool handles (brown)	M	1 rectangle, 1" × 4"	1 rectangle, 1½" × 7½"
	N	1 rectangle, 1" × 2¾"	1 rectangle, 1½" × 5"
Tool tops (gray dot)	O	1 rectangle, 1½" × 3¾"	1 rectangle, 2½" × 7"
	P	4 rectangles, ¾" × 2¼"	4 rectangles, 1" × 4"
	Q	1 rectangle, ¾" × 3½"	1 rectangle, 1" × 6½"
	R	2 squares, 1" × 1"	2 squares, 1½" × 1½"
Tool top (gray floral)	S	1 rectangle, 1½" × 3¾"	1 rectangle, 2½" × 7"

MAKING THE BLOCK

Instructions are for both 6" and 12" blocks. Sew all pieces right sides together. When layering pieces marked with a diagonal line, stitch on the marked line. Trim the seam allowances to ¼". Press all seam allowances open to reduce bulk.

1. Draw a diagonal line on the wrong side of the B squares. Sew B to the top-left corner of S. Sew B to the top-right corner of O. Join the S and O units to make the spade unit.

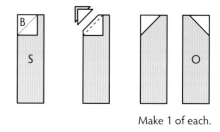

Make 1 of each.

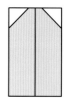

Make 1 unit.

2. Sew R between the C rectangles to make the spade-handle top. Sew N between the D rectangles to make the spade-handle bottom. Join the top and bottom handles to make the spade-handle unit.

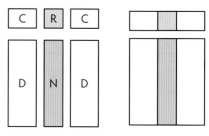

Make 1 unit.

3. Join the spade and handle units. Sew A and E to the sides of the unit to make the spade section.

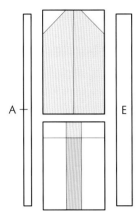

Make 1 section.

4. Draw a diagonal line on the wrong side of the K squares. Sew K to one end of P to make a prong unit. Make two prong units and two reversed.

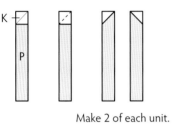

Make 2 of each unit.

5. Join the prong units, I, and L. Sew Q to the unit to make the rake top.

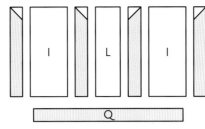

Make 1 unit.

6. Sew R between F rectangles to make the handle top.

Make 1 unit.

7. Join the handle top to the rake top. Add J to make the rake unit.

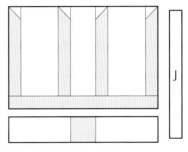

Make 1 unit.

8. Sew M between G and H to make the rake handle. Join the rake handle and rake top to make the rake section.

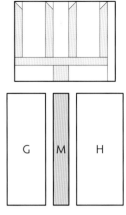

Make 1 section.

9. Join the spade and rake sections to make the block.

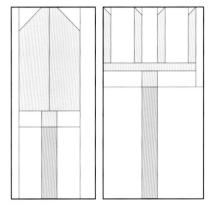

Garden Tools block

Choosing Fabrics

Medium- and small-scale fabrics are perfect for making blocks with smaller pieces! Small florals, polka dots, and ginghams are some of my absolute favorites. I love using them in blocks like the poppies, acorns, and grasshopper. Bee wings, butterfly wings, bird wings, and flower petals are great places to showcase your favorite large-scale prints and florals. Most importantly, have fun playing with your fabrics!

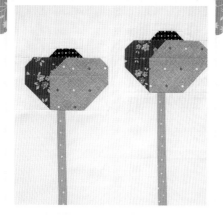

Poppies

FABRIC	PIECE	6" BLOCK	12" BLOCK
Background (white)	A	1 rectangle, 1¾" × 2¼"	1 rectangle, 3" × 4"
	B	1 rectangle, 1½" × 2"	1 rectangle, 2½" × 3½"
	C	1 rectangle, 1¼" × 2¼"	1 rectangle, 2" × 4"
	D	1 rectangle, 1" × 2"	1 rectangle, 1½" × 3½"
	E	8 squares, ¾" × ¾"	8 squares, 1" × 1"
	F	4 squares, 1¼" × 1¼"	4 squares, 2" × 2"
	G	1 rectangle, 2" × 3¼"	1 rectangle, 3½" × 6"
	H	1 rectangle, 1¾" × 3¼"	1 rectangle, 3" × 6"
	I	1 rectangle, 1½" × 3¾"	1 rectangle, 2½" × 7"
	J	1 rectangle, 1¾" × 3¾"	1 rectangle, 3" × 7"
	K	1 rectangle, 1" × 6½"	1 rectangle, 1½" × 12½"
	L	2 rectangles, 1¼" × 1¾"	2 rectangles, 2" × 3"
	M	1 square, 1½" × 1½"	1 square, 2½" × 2½"
Stems (green)	N	1 rectangle, ¾" × 3¼"	1 rectangle, 1" × 6"
	O	1 rectangle, ¾" × 3¾"	1 rectangle, 1" × 7"
Flower centers (black)	P	2 rectangles, ¾" × 1½"	2 rectangles, 1" × 2½"
Inner petals (red solid)	Q	2 squares, 1" × 1"	2 squares, 1½" × 1½"
Outer petals (pink)	R	2 squares, 1" × 1"	2 squares, 1½" × 1½"
	S	2 rectangles, 1" × 1¾"	2 rectangles, 1½" × 3"
	T	2 rectangles, 1½" × 2¼"	2 rectangles, 2½" × 4"
Middle petals (red floral)	U	2 rectangles, 1" × 1¼"	2 rectangles, 1½" × 2"
	V	2 rectangles, 1¼" × 1½"	2 rectangles, 2" × 2½"
	W	2 squares, 1" × 1"	2 squares, 1½" × 1½"

MAKING THE BLOCK

Instructions are for both 6" and 12" blocks. Sew all pieces right sides together. When layering pieces marked with a diagonal line, stitch on the marked line. Trim the seam allowances to ¼". Press all seam allowances open to reduce bulk.

1. Draw a diagonal line on the wrong side of the R and W squares. Sew W to Q. Sew R to the Q unit, placing the marked line perpendicular to the seam. Make two units.

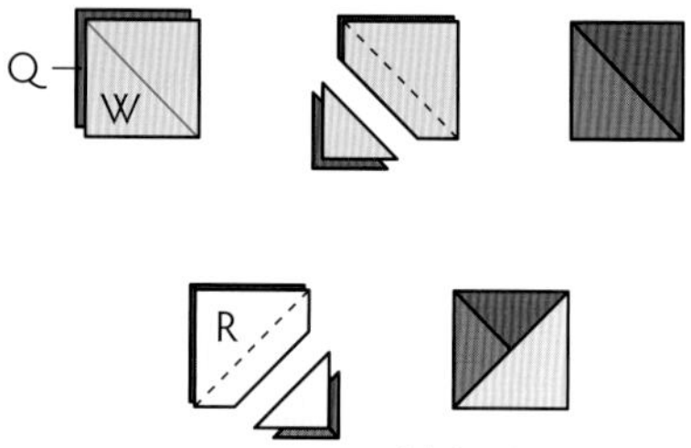

Make 2 units.

2. Draw a diagonal line on the wrong side of the E squares. Sew E to the top-left corner of U. Make two units.

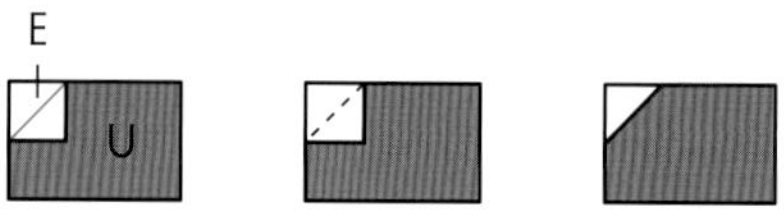

Make 2 units.

3. Sew E to the top-right corner of S. Make two units.

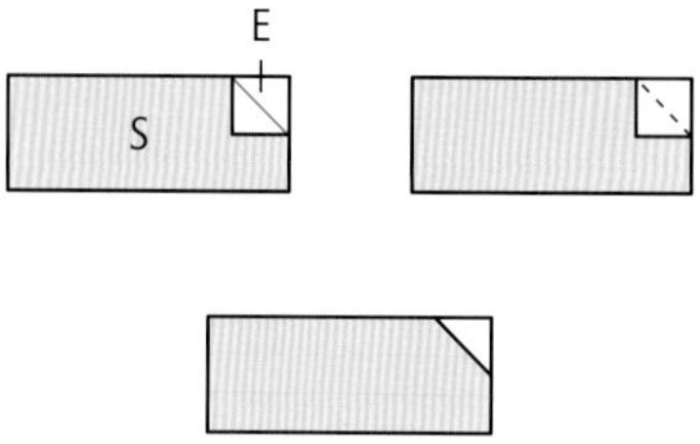

Make 2 units.

4. Join one of each unit from steps 1–3 to make the top-poppy unit. Make two units.

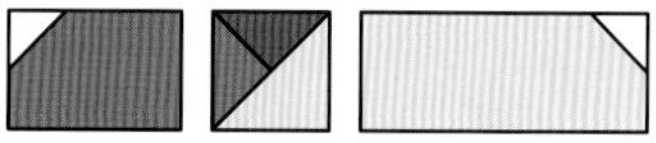

Make 2 units.

5. Draw a diagonal line on the wrong side of the F squares. Sew F to one end of V. Make two units.

Make 2 units.

6. Sew F on the bottom-right corner of T. Make two units.

 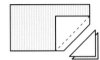

Make 2 units.

7. Join V and T units to make the bottom-poppy unit. Join the top- and bottom-poppy units. Make two flower units.

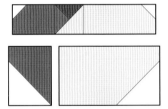

Make 2 units.

8. Sew E to each end of P. Make two P units.

Make 2 units.

9. Sew A, B, and C to one P unit to make the left-flower center.

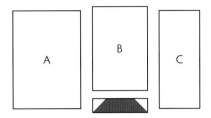

Make 1 unit.

10. Join G, N, and H to make a stem. Join D, the left-flower center, a flower, and stem to make the left poppy.

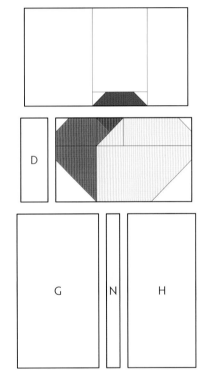

Make 1 unit.

11. Join L and M to the remaining P unit to make the right-flower center.

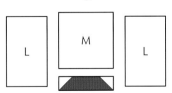

Make 1 unit.

12. Join I, O, and J to make a stem. Join the right-flower center, the remaining flower, and the stem to make the right poppy.

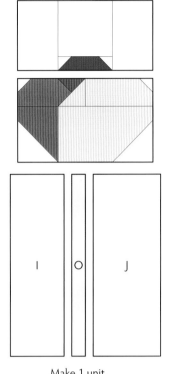

Make 1 unit.

13. Sew K between the left and right poppies to make the block.

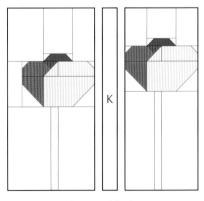

Poppies block

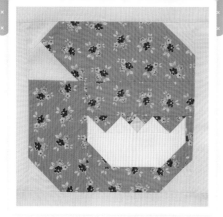

Lily Pad

FABRIC	PIECE	6" BLOCK	12" BLOCK
Background (light blue)	A	2 rectangles, 1" × 6½"	2 rectangles, 1½" × 12½"
	B	2 rectangles, 1" × 5½"	2 rectangles, 1½" × 10½"
	C	4 squares, 1½" × 1½"	4 squares, 2½" × 2½"
	D	1 square, 2" × 2"	1 square, 3½" × 3½"
Lily pad (green)	E	2 squares, 1" × 1"	2 squares, 1½" × 1½"
	F	1 rectangle, 2¼" × 5½"	1 rectangle, 4" × 10½"
	G	1 rectangle, 2¼" × 3¾"	1 rectangle, 4" × 7"
	H	1 rectangle, 1½" × 3¾"	1 rectangle, 2½" × 7"
	I	1 rectangle, 1¼" × 3¾"	1 rectangle, 2" × 7"
	J	1 rectangle, ¾" × 2"	1 rectangle, 1" × 3½"
	K	2 squares, 1¼" × 1¼"	2 squares, 2" × 2"
	L	2 rectangles, 1" × 1½"	2 rectangles, 1½" × 2½"
Flower (pink)	M	1 rectangle, 1½" × 3½"	1 rectangle, 2½" × 6½"
	N	6 squares, 1" × 1"	6 squares, 1½" × 1½"
Flower center (yellow)	O	1 rectangle, 1" × 1½"	1 rectangle, 1½" × 2½"

MAKING THE BLOCK

Instructions are for both 6" and 12" blocks. Sew all pieces right sides together. When layering pieces marked with a diagonal line, stitch on the marked line. Trim the seam allowances to ¼". Press all seam allowances open to reduce bulk.

1. Draw a diagonal line on the wrong side of the C and D squares. Sew D to the bottom-left corner of F. Sew C to the top-left and top-right corners of F to make the F unit.

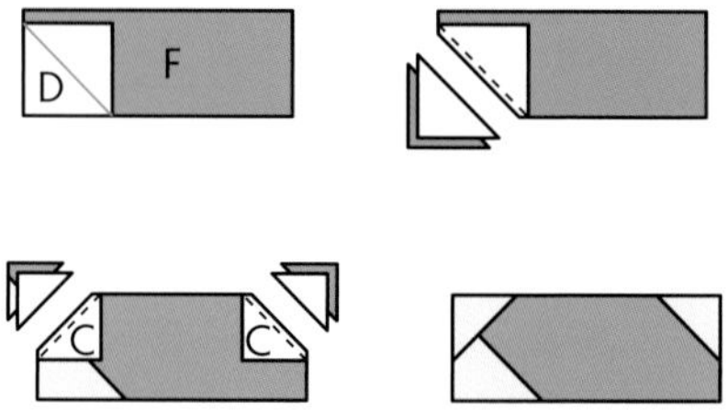

Make 1 unit.

2. Sew C to the bottom-left corner of G to make the G unit.

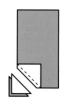

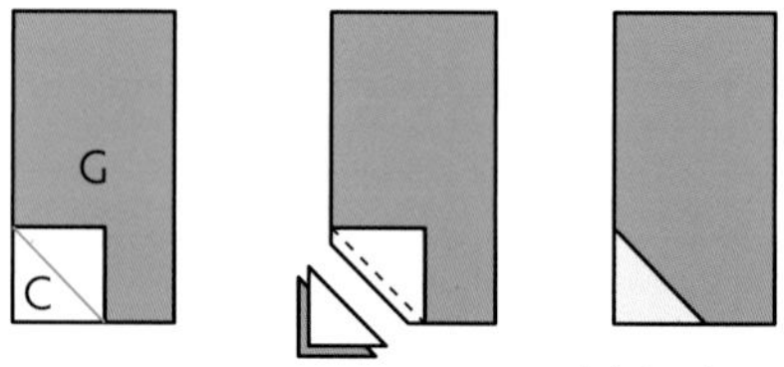

Make 1 unit.

3. Draw a diagonal line on the wrong side of the N squares. Sew N to each end of L. Make two L units.

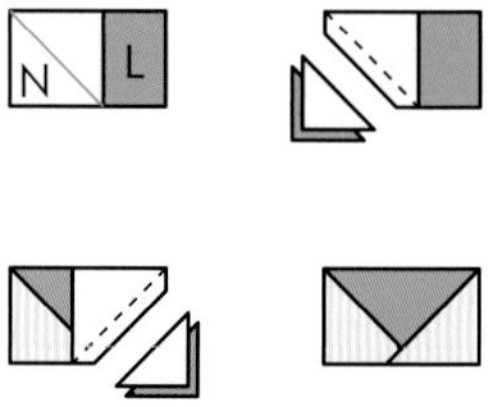

Make 2 units.

4. Draw a diagonal line on the wrong side of the E squares. Sew E to each end of O. Sew N to one end of O, placing the marked line perpendicular to the seam. Repeat to sew N to the other end of O to make the O unit.

Make 1 unit.

5. Join the L and O units to make the flower-center unit.

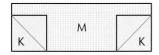

Make 1 unit.

6. Draw a diagonal line on the wrong side of the K squares. Sew K to the bottom-left and bottom-right corners of M to make the M unit.

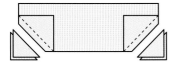

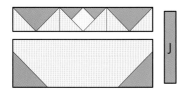

Make 1 unit.

7. Join the flower-center unit, M unit, and J to make the flower unit.

Make 1 unit.

8. Join H and I to the flower unit. Sew C to the bottom-right corner of the flower unit.

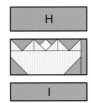

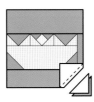

Make 1 unit.

9. Join units G and F to the flower unit to make the lily pad.

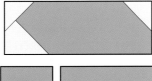

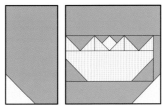

Make 1 unit.

10. Join B to the lily pad. Add A to make the block.

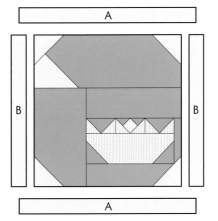

Lily Pad block

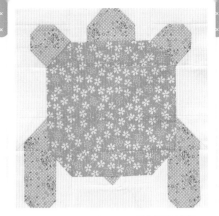

Turtle

FABRIC	PIECE	6" BLOCK	12" BLOCK
Background (white)	A	4 rectangles, 1" × 2¼"	4 rectangles, 1½" × 4"
	B	2 rectangles, 1" × 1½"	2 rectangles, 1½" × 2½"
	C	2 rectangles, 1" × 1¾"	2 rectangles, 1½" × 3"
	D	6 squares, 1" × 1"	6 squares, 1½" × 1½"
	E	8 squares, ¾" × ¾"	8 squares, 1" × 1"
	F	2 rectangles, 1½" × 2"	2 rectangles, 2½" × 3½"
	G	2 squares, 1½" × 1½"	2 squares, 2½" × 2½"
	H	4 rectangles, ¾" × 1½"	4 rectangles, 1" × 2½"
	I	2 rectangles, ¾" × 2¼"	2 rectangles, 1" × 4"
	J	1 rectangle, 1¼" × 3"	1 rectangle, 2" × 5½"
Head and legs (aqua)	K	1 rectangle, 1½" × 2"	1 rectangle, 2½" × 3½"
	L	2 squares, 1¾" × 1¾"	2 squares, 3" × 3"
	M	2 rectangles, 1¼" × 1½"	2 rectangles, 2" × 2½"
	N	2 rectangles, 1½" × 2¼"	2 rectangles, 2½" × 4"
	O	1 rectangle, ¾" × 1"	1 rectangle, 1" × 1½"
Turtle shell (green)	P	4 squares, 1¼" × 1¼"	4 squares, 2" × 2"
	Q	2 rectangles, 1¼" × 3"	2 rectangles, 2" × 5½"
	R	1 rectangle, 2" × 4½"	1 rectangle, 3½" × 8½"
	S	1 rectangle, 1½" × 4½"	1 rectangle, 2½" × 8½"

MAKING THE BLOCK

Instructions are for both 6" and 12" blocks. Sew all pieces right sides together. When layering pieces marked with a diagonal line, stitch on the marked line. Trim the seam allowances to ¼". Press all seam allowances open to reduce bulk.

1. Draw a diagonal line on the wrong side of the D squares. Sew D to the top-left and top-right corners of K to make the K unit.

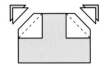

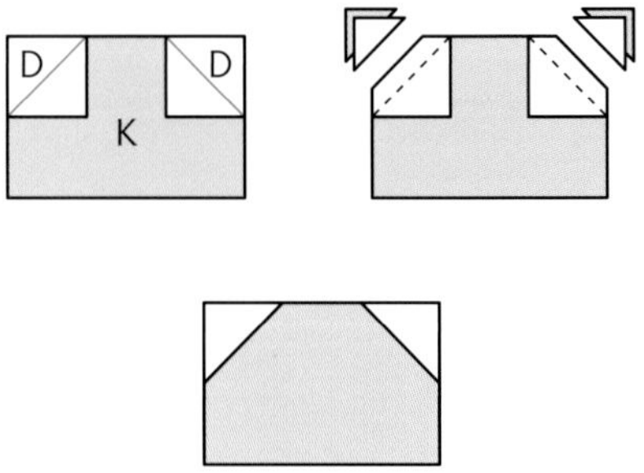

Make 1 unit.

2. Sew the K unit between B rectangles. Add Q to make the head unit.

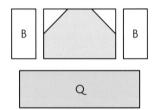

Make 1 unit.

3. Draw a diagonal line on the wrong side of the E and P squares. Sew D to opposite corners of L. Sew E and P to the remaining corners of L. Make two L units.

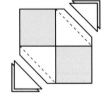

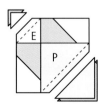

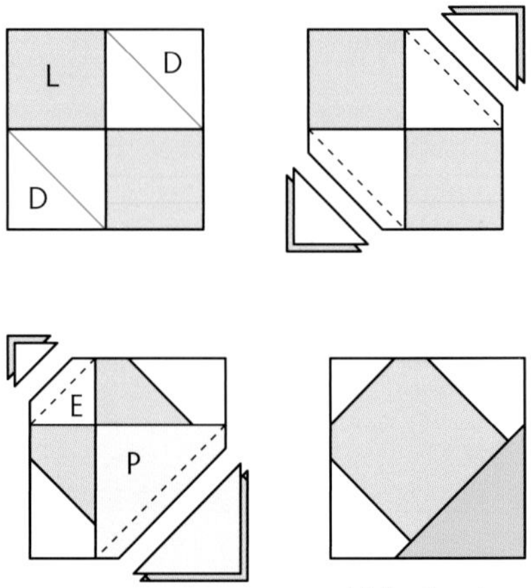

Make 2 units.

4. Sew C to an L unit. Sew A to the unit to make the front-leg unit. Make two units.

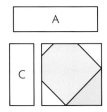

Make 2 units.

5. Join the front-leg and head units to make the top-turtle unit.

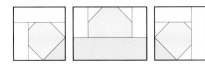

Make 1 unit.

6. Sew R between F rectangles to make the middle-turtle unit.

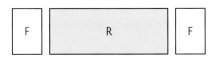

Make 1 unit.

7. Sew H to M. Repeat to make two M units. Draw a diagonal line on the wrong side of the G squares. Sew G to the top of an M unit, making sure the marked line crosses the seamline. Make one G unit and one reversed.

Make 1 of each unit.

8. Sew a G unit to each end of S to make the S unit.

Make 1 unit.

9. Sew E to the bottom-left and bottom-right corners of N. Make two N units.

Make 2 units.

10. Sew A and I to an N unit to make a back-leg unit. Repeat to make a reversed back-leg unit.

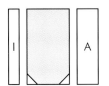

Make 1 of each unit.

11. Sew P to the top-right corner of a back-leg unit. Sew P to the top-left corner of the reversed back-leg unit.

 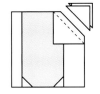

Make 1 of each unit.

12. Sew E to each end of O to make the O unit.

Make 1 unit.

13. Sew the O unit between two H rectangles to make the H/O unit. Sew Q and J to the H/O unit to make the tail unit.

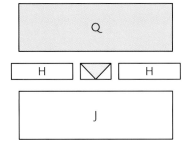

Make 1 unit.

14. Join the back-leg units to the tail unit. Add the S unit to make the bottom-turtle unit.

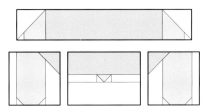

Make 1 unit.

15. Join the top-turtle, middle-turtle, and bottom-turtle units to make the block.

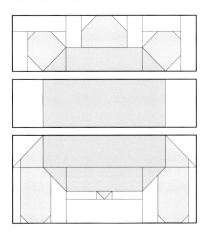

Turtle block

Duck

FABRIC	PIECE	6" BLOCK	12" BLOCK
Background (white)	A	1 rectangle, 2¼" × 4¼"	1 rectangle, 4" × 8"
	B	1 square, 2" × 2"	1 square, 3½" × 3½"
	C	1 rectangle, 1" × 1¾"	1 rectangle, 1½" × 3"
	D	1 rectangle, ¾" × 2¾"	1 rectangle, 1" × 5"
	E	2 squares, ¾" × ¾"	2 squares, 1" × 1"
	F	2 squares, 1¼" × 1¼"	2 squares, 2" × 2"
	G	1 square, 1½" × 1½"	1 square, 2½" × 2½"
	H	1 rectangle, 1¼" × 1½"	1 rectangle, 2" × 2½"
	I	1 rectangle, 1¼" × 1¾"	1 rectangle, 2" × 3"
	J	1 rectangle, 1" × 2¾"	1 rectangle, 1½" × 5"
	K	1 rectangle, 1" × 3½"	1 rectangle, 1½" × 6½"
Water (blue)	L	1 rectangle, 2½" × 6½"	1 rectangle, 4½" × 12½"
Beak (orange)	M	1 rectangle, 1¼" × 1½"	1 rectangle, 2" × 2½"
Wing (light orange)	N	1 rectangle, 1½" × 2½"	1 rectangle, 2½" × 4½"
	O	1 square, 2½" × 2½"	1 square, 4½" × 4½"
Duck (yellow)	P	1 rectangle, 1½" × 2"	1 rectangle, 2½" × 3½"
	Q	1 rectangle, 1" × 1½"	1 rectangle, 1½" × 2½"
	R	3 squares, 1" × 1"	3 squares, 1½" × 1½"
	S	1 rectangle, 2" × 3½"	1 rectangle, 3½" × 6½"
	T	1 square, ¾" × ¾"	1 square, 1" × 1"
	U	1 rectangle, 1¼" × 2¾"	1 rectangle, 2" × 5"
	V	1 rectangle, ¾" × 4½"	1 rectangle, 1" × 8½"

MAKING THE BLOCK

Instructions are for both 6" and 12" blocks. Sew all pieces right sides together. When layering pieces marked with a diagonal line, stitch on the marked line. Trim the seam allowances to ¼". Press all seam allowances open to reduce bulk.

1. Draw a diagonal line on the wrong side of the E squares. Sew E to the top-right corner of P. Sew M and D to the unit to make the head unit.

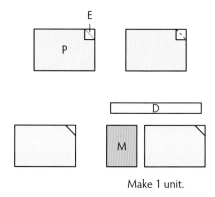

Make 1 unit.

2. Draw a diagonal line on the wrong side of the T square. Sew T to the top-right corner of C. Sew Q to the unit to make the neck unit.

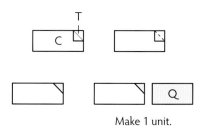

Make 1 unit.

3. Join the neck and head units. Draw a diagonal line on the wrong side of the B square. Sew B to the top-left corner of the neck/head unit to make the duck-head unit.

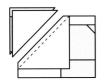

Make 1 unit.

4. Sew the duck-head unit to A to make the duck-top section.

Make 1 section.

5. Draw a diagonal line on the wrong side of the F squares. Sew F to the top-left corner and a marked E to the bottom-left corner of U to make the duck-front unit.

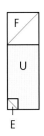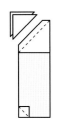

Make 1 unit.

6. Draw a diagonal line on the wrong side of the R squares. Sew R to the top-left and bottom-left corners of N to make the N unit.

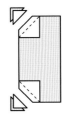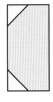

Make 1 unit.

7. Sew K to S. Draw a diagonal line on the wrong side of the O square. Sew O to the K/S unit.

Make 1 unit.

8. Sew the N unit to the K/S unit. Add V to make the wing unit. Draw a diagonal line on the wrong side of the G square. Sew G to the top-right corner and F to the bottom-right corner of the wing unit.

Make 1 unit.

9. Sew R to the top-left corner of I to make the tail unit.

Make 1 unit.

10. Join the duck-front unit, wing unit, tail unit, J, and H to make the duck-body section.

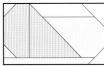

Make 1 section.

11. Join the duck-top section, duck-body section, and L to make the block.

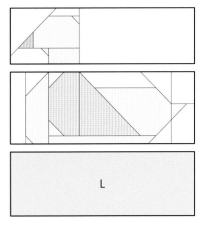

Duck block

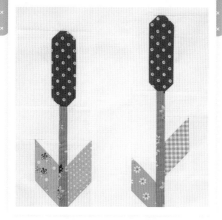

Cattails

FABRIC	PIECE	6" BLOCK	12" BLOCK
Background (white)	A	1 rectangle, 1¾" × 6½"	1 rectangle, 3" × 12½"
	B	1 rectangle, ¾" × 3"	1 rectangle, 1" × 5½"
	C	1 rectangle, 1¼" × 2¾"	1 rectangle, 2" × 5"
	D	1 rectangle, 1½" × 2¾"	1 rectangle, 2½" × 5"
	E	1 rectangle, 1¾" × 2¾"	1 rectangle, 3" × 5"
	F	2 rectangles, 1" × 2¾"	2 rectangles, 1½" × 5"
	G	8 squares, ¾" × ¾"	8 squares, 1" × 1"
	H	1 rectangle, 1½" × 1¾"	1 rectangle, 2½" × 3"
	I	1 rectangle, 1¼" × 1½"	1 rectangle, 2" × 2½"
	J	1 rectangle, 1¼" × 2"	1 rectangle, 2" × 3½"
	K	1 rectangle, 1¼" × 2¼"	1 rectangle, 2" × 4"
	L	1 rectangle, 1½" × 2"	1 rectangle, 2½" × 3½"
	M	1 rectangle, 1" × 2½"	1 rectangle, 1½" × 4½"
	N	7 squares, 1¼" × 1¼"	7 squares, 2" × 2"
	O	1 square, 1" × 1"	1 square, 1½" × 1½"
	P	1 rectangle, 1¼" × 2½"	1 rectangle, 2" × 4½"
Leaves and stems (assorted greens)	Q	2 rectangles, 1¼" × 2½"	2 rectangles, 2" × 4½"
	R	1 rectangle, 1¼" × 2"	1 rectangle, 2" × 3½"
	S	1 rectangle, 1¼" × 2¼"	1 rectangle, 2" × 4"
	T	1 rectangle, ¾" × 4"	1 rectangle, 1" × 7½"
	U	1 rectangle, ¾" × 3½"	1 rectangle, 1" × 6½"
Cattail tops (brown)	V	2 rectangles, 1¼" × 2¾"	2 rectangles, 2" × 5"

MAKING THE BLOCK

Instructions are for both 6" and 12" blocks. Sew all pieces right sides together. When layering pieces marked with a diagonal line, stitch on the marked line. Trim the seam allowances to ¼". Press all seam allowances open to reduce bulk.

1. Draw a diagonal line on the wrong side of the G squares. Sew G to opposite corners of V. Repeat to sew G to each remaining corner of V. Make two V units.

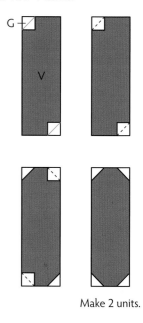

Make 2 units.

2. Sew one V unit between D and F. Add C for the left cattail-top unit.

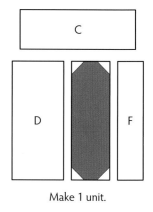

Make 1 unit.

3. Draw a diagonal line on the wrong side of the N squares. Sew N to each end of Q, making sure to orient the marked lines in the same direction. Make one leaf unit and one reversed.

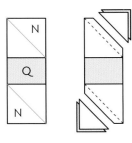

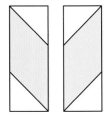

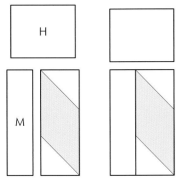

Make 1 of each unit.

4. Sew M and H to one leaf unit to make the left leaf.

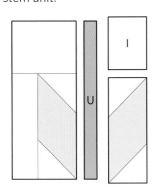

Make 1 unit.

5. Sew I to the reversed leaf unit to make the right leaf. Sew U between the left and right leaves to make the left-stem unit.

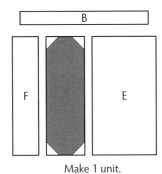

Make 1 unit.

6. Sew the remaining V unit between F and E. Add B to make the right cattail-top unit.

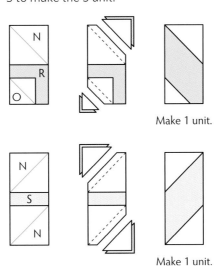

Make 1 unit.

7. Draw a diagonal line on the wrong side of the O square. Sew O to the bottom-left corner and N to the top-right corner of R to make the R unit. Repeat to sew N to each end of S to make the S unit.

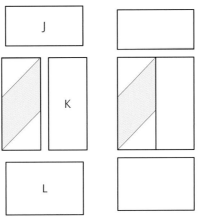

Make 1 unit.

Make 1 unit.

8. Sew K to the S unit. Add J and L to make the right leaf.

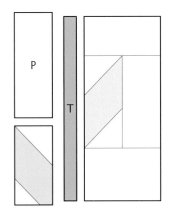

Make 1 unit.

9. Join P to the R unit from step 7 to make the left leaf. Sew T between the left and right leaves to make the right-stem unit.

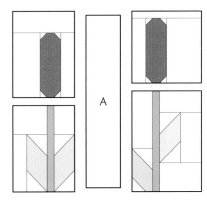

Make 1 unit.

10. Join the left cattail-top and stem units to make the left cattail. Join the right cattail-top and stem units to make the right cattail. Sew A between the left and right cattail units to make the block.

Cattails block

MAKING THE BLOCK

Instructions are for both 6" and 12" blocks. Sew all pieces right sides together. When layering pieces marked with a diagonal line, stitch on the marked line. Trim the seam allowances to ¼". Press all seam allowances open to reduce bulk.

1. Draw a diagonal line on the wrong side of the S squares. Sew S to one corner of V. Sew S to two remaining corners of V. Make two V units.

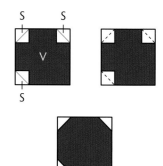

Make 2 units.

2. Sew T and U to a V unit. Make two. Draw a diagonal line on the wrong side of L. Sew L to the corners of unit V. Make two units.

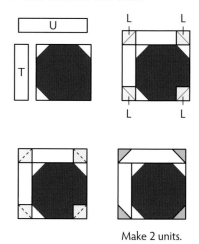

Make 2 units.

FABRIC	PIECE	6" BLOCK	12" BLOCK
Background (white)	A	1 rectangle, ¾" × 6½"	1 rectangle, 1" × 12½"
	B	9 squares, 1" × 1"	9 squares, 1½" × 1½"
	C	2 rectangles, 1¼" × 2"	2 rectangles, 2" × 3½"
	D	4 rectangles, 1" × 1¾"	4 rectangles, 1½" × 3"
	E	4 squares, ¾" × ¾"	4 squares, 1" × 1"
	F	2 squares, 1¼" × 1¼"	2 squares, 2" × 2"
	G	2 rectangles, ¾" × 2¾"	2 rectangles, 1" × 5"
Frog legs and mouth (light green)	H	1 rectangle, 1¼" × 5½"	1 rectangle, 2" × 10½"
	I	2 rectangles, 1½" × 2¾"	2 rectangles, 2½" × 5"
	J	2 rectangles, ¾" × 1¾"	2 rectangles, 1" × 3"
	K	2 squares, 1" × 1"	2 squares, 1½" × 1½"
Frog head and body (dark green)	L	8 squares, ¾" × ¾"	8 squares, 1" × 1"
	M	1 rectangle, 3½" × 4"	1 rectangle, 6½" × 7½"
	N	1 rectangle, 1" × 5½"	1 rectangle, 1½" × 10½"
	O	1 rectangle, 1" × 1½"	1 rectangle, 1½" × 2½"
	P	2 rectangles, 1" × 1¾"	2 rectangles, 1½" × 3"
	Q	2 rectangles, ¾" × 1¾"	2 rectangles, 1" × 3"
	R	2 rectangles, ¾" × 2½"	2 rectangles, 1" × 4½"
Eyes (white)	S	6 squares, ¾" × ¾"	6 squares, 1" × 1"
	T	2 rectangles, ¾" × 1½"	2 rectangles, 1" × 2½"
	U	2 rectangles, ¾" × 1¾"	2 rectangles, 1" × 3"
Eyes (black)	V	2 squares, 1½" × 1½"	2 squares, 2½" × 2½"

3. Sew a unit from step 2 between Q and P. Add R to make an R unit. Repeat to make a reversed R unit.

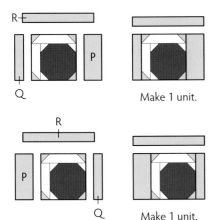

Make 1 unit.

Make 1 unit.

4. Draw a diagonal line on the wrong side of eight B squares. Sew B to the top-left and top-right corners of an R unit. Make one of each eye unit.

Make 1 unit.

Make 1 unit.

5. Sew the unmarked B to O. Sew the B/O unit between the eye units to make the eye section. Sew the eye section between C rectangles. Add A to make the frog-top section.

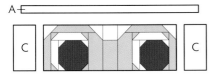

Make 1 section.

6. Join N and H. Draw a diagonal line on the wrong side of the E and F squares. Sew E to the top-left and top-right corners of the unit. Sew F to the bottom-left and bottom-right corners to make the mouth unit. Sew the mouth unit between D rectangles to make the frog-middle section.

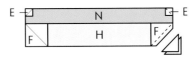

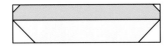

Make 1 section.

7. Draw a diagonal line on the wrong side of the K squares. Sew K to the bottom-left and bottom-right corners of M to make the M unit.

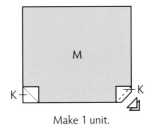

Make 1 unit.

8. Stitch B to the top-right and bottom-left corners of I. Sew E to the top-left corner of I. Sew B and E on another I, reversing the position of the marked squares. Make one of each I unit.

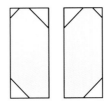

Make 1 of each unit.

9. Sew G to an I unit. Sew D and J to the unit. Make one leg unit and one reversed.

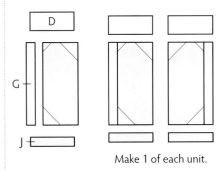

Make 1 of each unit.

10. Sew a leg unit to each side of the M unit to make the frog-bottom section.

Make 1 section.

11. Join the frog-top, -middle, and -bottom sections to make the block.

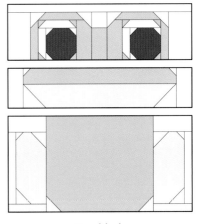

Frog block

Gone Fishing

FABRIC	PIECE	6" BLOCK	12" BLOCK
Background (white)	A	1 rectangle, ¾" × 6½"	1 rectangle, 1" × 12½"
	B	1 rectangle, 1" × 3"	1 rectangle, 1½" × 5½"
	C	4 squares, 1¼" × 1¼"	4 squares, 2" × 2"
	D	2 squares, 1½" × 1½"	2 squares, 2½" × 2½"
	E	2 rectangles, 1" × 1¾"	2 rectangles, 1½" × 3"
	F	2 rectangles, 1¼" × 2¼"	2 rectangles, 2" × 4"
	G	1 rectangle, 1" × 2"	1 rectangle, 1½" × 3½"
	H	2 rectangles, 1" × 3¾"	2 rectangles, 1½" × 7"
	I	12 squares, ¾" × ¾"	12 squares, 1" × 1"
	J	6 rectangles, ¾" × 1"	6 rectangles, 1" × 1½"
	K	2 rectangles, ¾" × 2"	2 rectangles, 1" × 3½"
	L	2 rectangles, 1½" × 2¼"	2 rectangles, 2½" × 4"
	M	1 rectangle, 1¾" × 2"	1 rectangle, 3" × 3½"
Bobber centers (white/cream)	N	3 rectangles, 1" × 2"	3 rectangles, 1½" × 3½"
Bobber tops and bottoms (red)	O	3 rectangles, ¾" × 1"	3 rectangles, 1" × 1½"
	P	3 rectangles, 1¼" × 2"	3 rectangles, 2" × 3½"
Fins (green)	Q	1 rectangle, 1¼" × 3"	1 rectangle, 2" × 5½"
	R	1 rectangle, 1¼" × 2"	1 rectangle, 2" × 3½"
Fish (light blue)	S	2 rectangles, 2¼" × 3"	2 rectangles, 4" × 5½"
	T	2 rectangles, 1" × 1¼"	2 rectangles, 1½" × 2"
	U	2 squares, 1¼" × 1¼"	2 squares, 2" × 2"
	V	1 square, ¾" × ¾"	1 square, 1" × 1"

MAKING THE BLOCK

Instructions are for both 6" and 12" blocks. Sew all pieces right sides together. When layering pieces marked with a diagonal line, stitch on the marked line. Trim the seam allowances to ¼". Press all seam allowances open to reduce bulk.

1. Draw a diagonal line on the wrong side of the C squares. Sew C to each end of Q. Join B to the unit to make the back-fin unit.

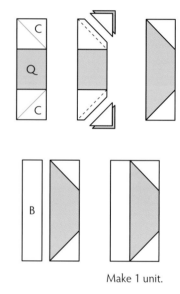

Make 1 unit.

2. Sew C to the top-left and bottom-left corners of S to make the S unit.

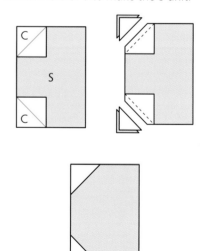

Make 1 unit.

3. Draw a diagonal line on the wrong side of the U squares. Sew U to each end of R to make the side-fin unit.

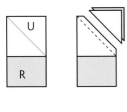

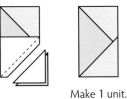

Make 1 unit.

4. Draw a diagonal line on the wrong side of the D squares. Sew D to the top-right and bottom-right corners of the remaining S.

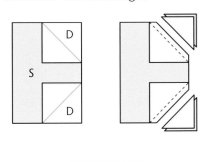

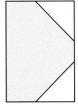

Make 1 unit.

5. Draw a diagonal line on the wrong side of the V square. Sew V to the top-right corner of an E. Sew the unit to the remaining E to make the mouth unit.

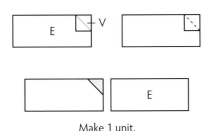

Make 1 unit.

6. Join T and the units from steps 1–5 to make the fish section.

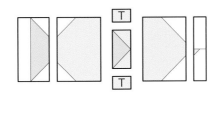

Make 1 section.

7. Sew O between J rectangles to make the bobber-top unit. Make three units.

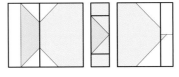

Make 3 units.

8. Join N and P. Draw a diagonal line on the wrong side of the I squares. Sew I to each corner of the unit. Make three bobber-bottom units.

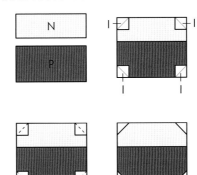

Make 3 units.

9. Join a bobber-top and bobber-bottom unit to make the bobber unit. Make three units.

Make 3 units.

10. Sew a K to a bobber unit. Sew F and L to the unit to make a bobber section. Make one left and one right bobber section.

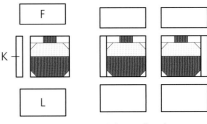

Make 1 of each section.

11. Join G and M to the remaining bobber unit to make the middle bobber section.

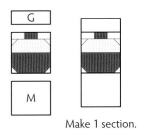

Make 1 section.

12. Join H rectangles and the bobber sections to make a three-bobber section.

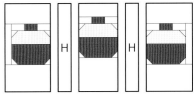

Make 1 section.

13. Join A, the fish, and three-bobber sections to make the block.

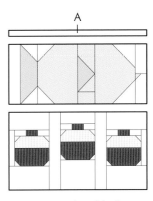

Gone Fishing block

Bear Paws

FABRIC	PIECE	6" BLOCK	12" BLOCK
Background (white)	A	4 rectangles, 2" × 2¾"	4 rectangles, 3½" × 5"
	B	20 squares, 1¼" × 1¼"	20 squares, 2" × 2"
Bear paw (brown)	C	4 squares, 2" × 2"	4 squares, 3½" × 3½"
	D	16 squares, 1¼" × 1¼"	16 squares, 2" × 2"
Center (pink)	E	1 square, 2" × 2"	1 square, 3½" × 3½"

MAKING THE BLOCK

Instructions are for both 6" and 12" blocks. Sew all pieces right sides together. When layering pieces marked with a diagonal line, stitch on the marked line. Trim the seam allowances to ¼". Press all seam allowances open to reduce bulk.

1. Draw a diagonal line on the wrong side of 16 B squares. Sew B to D. Make 16 D units.

Make 16 units.

2. Join an unmarked B and two D units. Join the remaining D units in pairs. Make four of each unit.

Make 4 units.

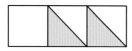

Make 4 units.

3. Sew one of each unit from step 2 to C to make a bear-paw unit. Make four units.

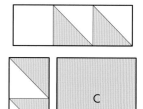

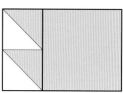

Make 4 units.

4. Join the bear-paw units, A, and E in rows. Sew the rows together to make the block.

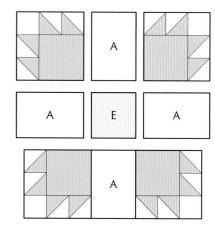

Bear Paws block

Mountain Lake

FABRIC	PIECE	6" BLOCK	12" BLOCK
Triangle squares (aqua)	A	1 square, 5" × 5"	1 square, 9½" × 9½"
	B	7 squares, 2" × 2"	7 squares, 3½" × 3½"
Background (white)	C	1 square, 5" × 5"	1 square, 9½" × 9½"
	D	7 squares, 2" × 2"	7 squares, 3½" × 3½"

MAKING THE BLOCK

Instructions are for both 6" and 12" blocks. Sew all pieces right sides together. When layering pieces marked with a diagonal line, stitch on the marked line. Trim the seam allowances to ¼". Press all seam allowances open to reduce bulk.

1. Draw a diagonal line on the wrong side of the A square. Sew A to C to make the A/C unit.

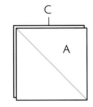

Make 1 unit.

2. Draw a diagonal line on the wrong side of the B squares. Sew B to D. Make seven B/D units.

Make 7 units.

3. Join three B/D units. Join four B/D units. Make one of each section.

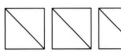

Make 1 section.

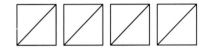

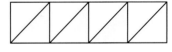

Make 1 section.

4. Sew the sections from step 3 to the A/C unit to make the block.

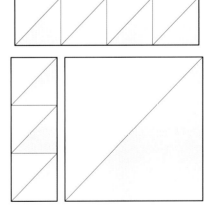

Mountain Lake block

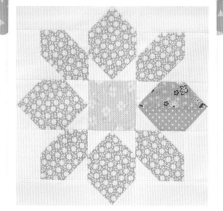

Wildflower

FABRIC	PIECE	6" BLOCK	12" BLOCK
Background (white)	A	4 rectangles, 1¼" × 2¾"	4 rectangles, 2" × 5"
	B	4 rectangles, 1¼" × 2"	4 rectangles, 2" × 3½"
	C	24 squares, 1¼" × 1¼"	24 squares, 2" × 2"
Flower petals (orange)	D	3 rectangles, 2" × 2¾"	3 rectangles, 3½" × 5"
	E	4 squares, 2" × 2"	4 squares, 3½" × 3½"
Center (yellow)	F	1 square, 2" × 2"	1 square, 3½" × 3½"
Leaf (green floral)	G	1 rectangle, 1¼" × 2¾"	1 rectangle, 2" × 5"
Leaf (green dot)	H	1 rectangle, 1¼" × 2¾"	1 rectangle, 2" × 5"

MAKING THE BLOCK

Instructions are for both 6" and 12" blocks. Sew all pieces right sides together. When layering pieces marked with a diagonal line, stitch on the marked line. Trim the seam allowances to ¼". Press all seam allowances open to reduce bulk.

1. Draw a diagonal line on the wrong side of the C squares. Sew C to the top-right and bottom-left corners of E. Make four E units.

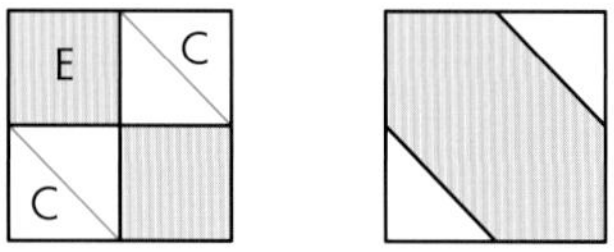

Make 4 units.

2. Sew B to an E unit. Sew A to the unit to make a corner unit. Make two corner units and two reversed.

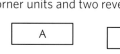

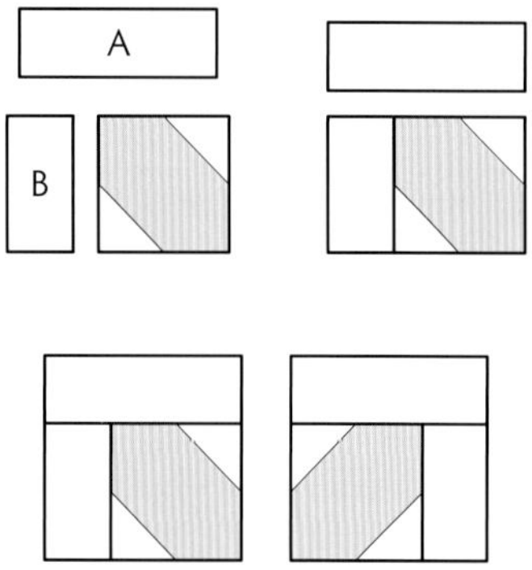

Make 2 of each unit.

3. Sew C to the top-left and bottom-right corners of D. Sew C to the remaining two corners of D. Make three side units.

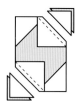

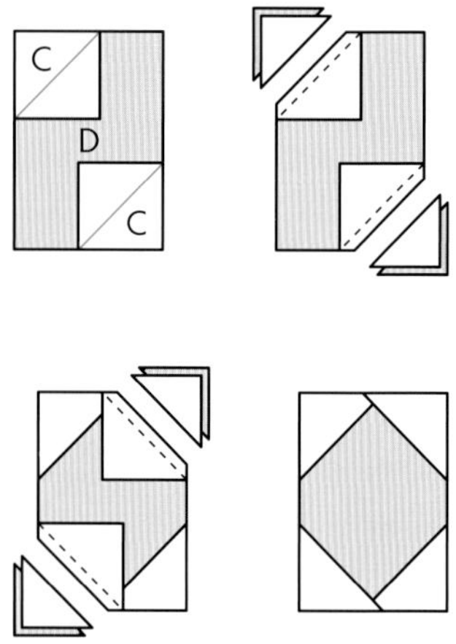

Make 3 units.

4. Join G and H. Repeat step 3 to sew C to the corners of the G/H unit to make the leaf unit.

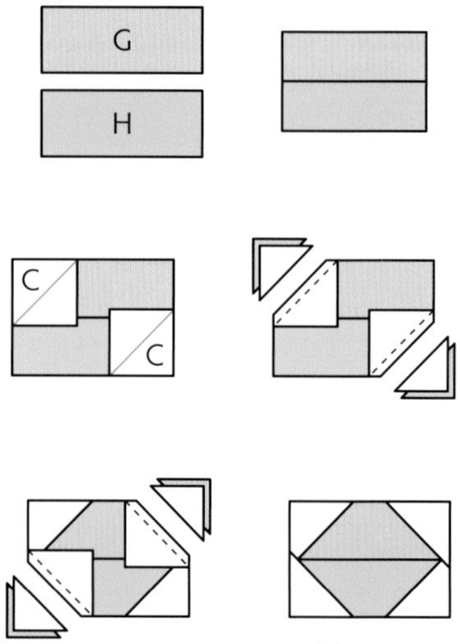

Make 1 unit.

5. Sew the corner units, side units, leaf unit, and F in rows. Join the rows to make the block.

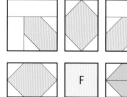

Wildflower block

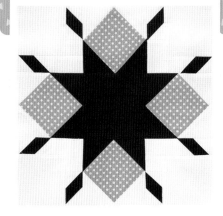

North Star

FABRIC	PIECE	6" BLOCK	12" BLOCK
Background (white)	A	4 squares, 2" × 2"	4 squares, 3½" × 3½"
	B	20 squares, 1" × 1"	20 squares, 1½" × 1½"
	C	4 rectangles, 1" × 1½"	4 rectangles, 1½" × 2½"
	D	8 squares, 1½" × 1½"	8 squares, 2½" × 2½"
Star accent (gray)	E	4 squares, 2½" × 2½"	4 squares, 4½" × 4½"
Star points (blue)	F	8 squares, 1½" × 1½"	8 squares, 2½" × 2½"
	G	8 rectangles, 1" × 1½"	8 rectangles, 1½" × 2½"
	H	1 square, 2½" × 2½"	1 square, 4½" × 4½"

MAKING THE BLOCK

Instructions are for both 6" and 12" blocks. Sew all pieces right sides together. When layering pieces marked with a diagonal line, stitch on the marked line. Trim the seam allowances to ¼". Press all seam allowances open to reduce bulk.

1. Draw a diagonal line on the wrong side of 16 B squares. Sew B to each end of G, making sure the marked lines are angled in the same direction. Sew B to each end of G, this time making sure to reverse the direction of the marked lines. Make four star-point units and four reversed.

Make 4 of each unit.

2. Sew B to one unit and C to one reversed. Make four B and four C.

Make 4 of each unit.

3. Join A, a B unit, and a C unit to make a corner unit. Make four units.

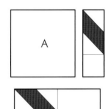

Make 4 units.

4. Draw a diagonal line on the wrong side of the D and F squares. Sew D to the top-left corner and F to the bottom-right corner of E. Sew D to the top-right corner and F to the bottom-left corner of E. Make four side units.

Make 4 units.

5. Sew the corner units, side units, and H square in rows. Join the rows to make the block.

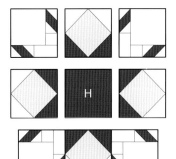

North Star block

Log Cabin

FABRIC	PIECE	6" BLOCK	12" BLOCK
Logs and center (13 assorted scraps)	A	1 square, 2" × 2"	1 square, 3½" × 3½"
	B	1 rectangle, 1¼" × 2"	1 rectangle, 2" × 3½"
	C	2 rectangles, 1¼" × 2¾"	2 rectangles, 2" × 5"
	D	2 rectangles, 1¼" × 3½"	2 rectangles, 2" × 6½"
	E	2 rectangles, 1¼" × 4¼"	2 rectangles, 2" × 8"
	F	2 rectangles, 1¼" × 5"	2 rectangles, 2" × 9½"
	G	2 rectangles, 1¼" × 5¾"	2 rectangles, 2" × 11"
	H	1 rectangle, 1¼" × 6½"	1 rectangle, 2" × 12½"

MAKING THE BLOCK

Instructions are for both 6" and 12" blocks. Sew all pieces right sides together. Trim the seam allowances to ¼". Press all seam allowances open to reduce bulk.

1. Sew B to the top of A to make the center unit. Sew C to the right side and then to the bottom of the unit.

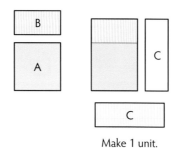

Make 1 unit.

2. Sew D to the left side and then to the top of the unit from step 1. Sew E to the right side and then to the bottom of the unit.

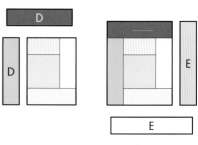

Make 1 unit.

3. Sew F to the left side and then to the top of the unit from step 2. Sew G to the right side and then to the bottom of the unit.

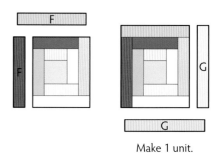

Make 1 unit.

4. Sew H to the left side of the unit from step 3 to make the block.

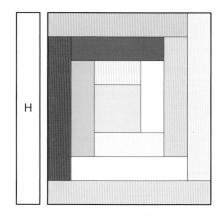

Log Cabin block

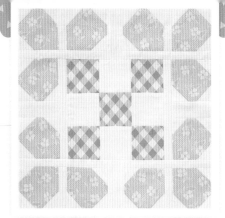

Honeybee

FABRIC	PIECE	6" BLOCK	12" BLOCK
Background (white)	A	4 squares, 1½" × 1½"	4 squares, 2½" × 2½"
	B	36 squares, 1" × 1"	36 squares, 1½" × 1½"
	C	4 rectangles, ¾" × 1¾"	4 rectangles, 1" × 3"
	D	2 rectangles, 1" × 2"	2 rectangles, 1½" × 3½"
	E	4 rectangles, ¾" × 3¼"	4 rectangles, 1" × 6"
	F	2 rectangles, ¾" × 3½"	2 rectangles, 1" × 6½"
	G	2 rectangles, 1" × 1¾"	2 rectangles, 1½" × 3"
Honeybees (yellow)	H	12 squares, 1¾" × 1¾"	12 squares, 3" × 3"
Nine Patch (orange plaid)	I	5 squares, 1½" × 1½"	5 squares, 2½" × 2½"

MAKING THE BLOCK

Instructions are for both 6" and 12" blocks. Sew all pieces right sides together. When layering pieces marked with a diagonal line, stitch on the marked line. Trim the seam allowances to ¼". Press all seam allowances open to reduce bulk.

1. Draw a diagonal line on the wrong side of the B squares. Sew B to the top-left corner of H. Sew B to the top-right and bottom-left corners of H. Make 12 H units.

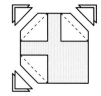

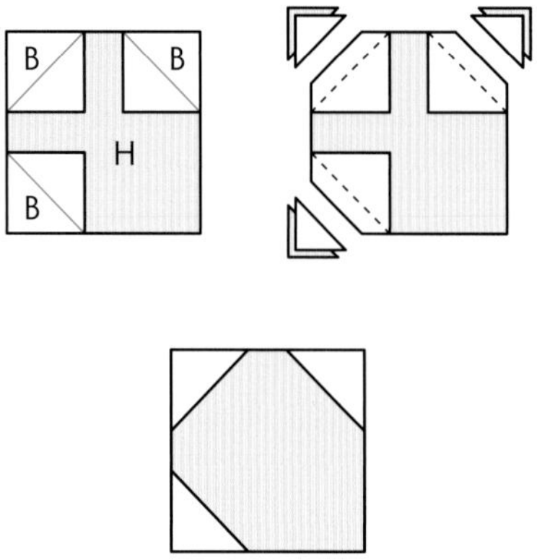

Make 12 units.

2. Sew C between two H units. Add E. Make four units.

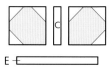

Make 4 units.

3. Sew D between two units from step 2. Make two rows.

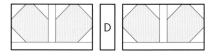

Make 2 rows.

4. Sew G between two H units. Add F to make a side unit. Make two.

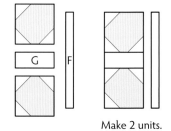

Make 2 units.

5. Join A and I squares to make a nine-patch unit.

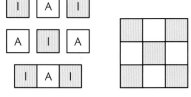

Make 1 unit.

6. Join the units to make the center row. Join the rows to make the block.

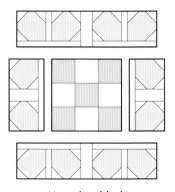

Honeybee block

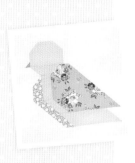

Acknowledgments

I want to acknowledge my great-grandma, Barbara-Lee Summers, who began our family quilting legacy, and my grandma, Rita Pickering, who taught me how to quilt and opened a whole new world to me.

A huge thank-you to Annie Seaboch (Annie Leigh's Sew Happy) for your beautiful long-arm quilting!

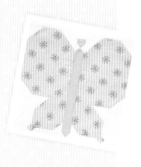

About the Author

Gracey Larson lives in beautiful, rural East Tennessee with her dad and mom, her two sisters, her brother, a bunny, and 10 chickens. When asked how long she has been a maker, Gracey says that she has been creating since she was old enough to hold a crayon. She has always enjoyed living in a world of color, pattern, and creativity. Gracey began quilting in 2009, after years of admiring her great-grandmother's quilts, and quilting has been an ongoing passion for her ever since.

As a Christian and self-described "wildflower," Gracey loves God, her family, her church family, adventure, traveling and singing with her family, and stitching those memories and moments into her quilts. Her patterns are unique and whimsical, and they appeal to a growing number of quilters who seek to include pictures in their own projects without the need for paper piecing or templates. Gracey's work has also appeared in *Love Patchwork & Quilting* magazine.